LIBERTY OF CONSCIENCE

The History of a Puritan Idea

L. John Van Til

PUBLISHING
PO BOX 817 • PHILLIPSBURG • NEW JERSEY 08865-0817

Copyright 1972
L. John Van Til

Van Til, L. John.
  Liberty of conscience : the history of a Puritan idea / L. John Van Til.
       p.   cm.
  Previously published: Nutley, N.J. : Craig Press, 1972.
  Includes bibliographical references.
  ISBN-10: 0-87552-460-5
  ISBN-13: 978-0-87552-460-3
  1. Liberty of conscience--History. I. Title.
BV741.V32   1992
323.44'2'09--dc20   91-45872

ABBREVIATIONS

S.P., Dom. Eliz.   Joseph Stevenson, *et al.*, eds., *Calendars of State Papers, Domestic Series, of the Reign of Elizabeth* (London, 1865 —).

Jordan, *Toleration*   W. K. Jordan, *The Development of Religious Toleration in England*, 4 vols. (Cambridge, 1932-1940).

D.N.B.   Leslie Stephen, *et al.*, eds., *Dictionary of National Biography*, 22 vols. (London, 1882-1949).

N.E.M.   Perry Miller, *The New England Mind*, 2 vols. (Boston, 1961).

CONTENTS

ABBREVIATIONS	iii
PREFACE	vii
INTRODUCTION	3

I. TOLERATION AND LIBERTY OF CONSCIENCE
   IN ELIZABETHAN ENGLAND — 4
   - A. The Elizabethan Government and the Problem of Conscience — 5
   - B. Elizabethan Puritans and the Problem of Conscience — 11
   - C. William Perkins: A Theology of Conscience — 16

II. TOLERATION AND LIBERTY OF CONSCIENCE
    IN OLD ENGLAND: 1600–40 — 29
   - A. Toleration Under the Early Stuarts: 1600–40 — 29
   - B. A Wider Acceptance of Liberty of Conscience: 1600–40 — 34
   - C. William Ames and the Problem of Conscience — 43
   - D. Conclusion — 51

III. CONSCIENCE AND THE BUILDERS
     OF THE BAY COLONY: 1630–40 — 55
   - A. Roger Williams — 58
   - B. The Antinomian Controversy: 1636–38 — 70
   - C. Conclusion — 80

IV. LIBERTY OF CONSCIENCE
    IN OLD ENGLAND: 1640–60 — 85
   - A. Liberty and Sovereignty in the Westminster Assembly — 86
   - B. Liberty of Conscience and the Leveller Movement — 95
   - C. Liberty of Conscience and the Policies of the Protectorate — 99
   - D. Conclusion — 104

V.	THE FAILURE OF LIBERTY OF CONSCIENCE IN RESTORATION ENGLAND	108
VI.	THE ACCEPTANCE OF LIBERTY OF CONSCIENCE IN AMERICA: 1630–1770	128
	A. Liberty of Conscience in the American Colonies: 1630–89	129
	B. Liberty, Sovereignty, and Revolutionary Ideology: 1689–1770	135
VII.	LIBERTY OF CONSCIENCE IN THE AMERICAN REVOLUTION	157
	A. Liberty and Sovereignty in the Constitutions of the New States	158
	B. Liberty of Conscience and the Declaration of Independence	164
	C. Liberty of Conscience and the Federal Constitution	168
VIII.	CONCLUSION	184
BIBLIOGRAPHY		187

PREFACE

Publication of a writing is always satisfying. Republication of a writing is especially satisfying for it indicates a degree of continued interest in the work. This study of liberty and conscience was first published twenty years ago and was produced with the support of a remarkable man—J. Howard Pew. I began this book just as I commenced working for him as a research assistant. He, indeed, was remarkable—as chairman of the board of Sun Oil, and as a very knowledgeable layman. Especially remarkable was his insight into the history of liberty. He was fond of saying that "from Christian freedom come all of our other freedoms." He was right. This study confirms that observation.

For the past twenty years I have been on the faculty of Grove City College, a fact, I would think, he would appreciate. J. Howard Pew called Grove City College "my school," and as such he dedicated himself to its growth and to the teaching of Christian values to its students. It was "his college" in at least two senses. He was graduated with the class of '00—the year 1900. J. Howard was also chairman of the college's board of trustees for decades, contributing generously to its building and operating funds.

This republication, then, becomes interesting in that it takes place with the warm support of Grove City College's sixth president, Jerry H. Combee, and its academic dean, Bill Anderson—both of whom appreciate freedom and liberty in the J. Howard Pew tradition. Any extended writing is always better with the help of thoughtful friends. My best friend, my wife, Kathryn Anne, was a vital part in ironing out language and insights when this book was originally created. Time has only enhanced her role in all my work. Sons Dirk Evan, Seth Jon, and Ethan Samuel have now grown to understand and appreciate liberty and freedom too. The efforts of the publishing staff at Presbyterian and Reformed are, of course, greatly appreciated as well.

LIBERTY
OF
CONSCIENCE

INTRODUCTION

Students of seventeenth-century England and America have long recognized the frequency of appeals to conscience in religious and political matters. William Perkins, an Elizabethan Puritan theologian, wrote volumes on the subject, much of which focused on his observation that Christ in the New Testament "hath given a liberty to conscience." Two centuries later, James Madison argued for a Bill of Rights in the first session of Congress, urging especially that this Bill of Rights should include provision for liberty of conscience because, he said, "the rights of conscience" is a subject about "which the people of America are most alarmed."

This study traces the development of liberty of conscience as a Puritan idea from Perkins to Madison and the Bill of Rights. Along the way many important people have their say, including Roger Williams, John Locke, Oliver Cromwell, James Madison, and others. One point that still seems especially important is the distinction between liberty of conscience and toleration. The point has been made time and again in the text, but here it may be noted that toleration is a grant from a government while liberty of conscience is an inherent condition of man given him when he was made in the image of God.

As this study is reissued, the nation marks the two-hundredth anniversary of the Bill of Rights. Strangely, very little has been said about the importance of the Bill of Rights; even less has been said about the religion clause of the First Amendment. If J. Howard Pew was correct in his observation that "from Christian freedom comes all of our other freedoms," more attention should be paid to the religion clause. As noted in the last chapter of this study, the religion clause is based squarely on the concept of Christian freedom as found in the Puritan tradition of liberty of conscience. Perhaps the republication of this study will help stimulate interest in ways to preserve and defend liberty and freedom.

Chapter I

TOLERATION AND LIBERTY OF CONSCIENCE IN ELIZABETHAN ENGLAND

Conscience was a familiar idea to Englishmen in the Age of Elizabeth. In the 1570's, for example, when the government found it necessary to tighten its control over Catholics, a member of Commons declared that conscience was "eternal, invisible, and not in the power of the greatest monarchy in the world."[1] The makers of government policy were not ignorant of the role of conscience, for the government stated its purpose was "not to have people molested by any inquisition or examination of their consciences in the causes of religion."[2] At the same time the English theologian, William Perkins, penned an extended treatise on conscience; in it he wrote, "God hath now in the New Testament given a liberty to the conscience."[3] The significance of conscience was not lost on Catholics either. As the Catholic problem continued to plague the Elizabethan government, Sir John Nevill, a Catholic, suggested that the needs of all concerned in the dispute could be resolved by a treaty that would provide for "a toleration through the realm to live with safety of conscience."[4]

All Elizabethans did not, however, use the idea of conscience in the same way. The examples cited illustrate two different attitudes toward the function of conscience in the affairs of men. On the one hand, the government's statement that it did not intend to examine consciences in matters of religion implied that it had the right to such an examination if it so desired. Consistent with this position was Sir John Nevill's statement, for he assumed that "safety of conscience" should be a matter of government policy, that is, part of a treaty. In contrast to this view of conscience stands that of the member of Parliament, claiming that conscience is not in the power of the greatest monarchy. In the same vein Perkins stated that God, not the crown or government, gave liberty to conscience. The difference represented in these two points of view was fundamental and irreconcilable. Elizabethan appeals to conscience, with few exceptions, were associated with the problem of the individual and his practice of religion. The two points of view noted reveal two different answers to the question of what the source of authority was in matters of religion. The government position assumed that exercise of conscience was a practice to be granted and tolerated by the crown or its agents. The member of Parliament and the theologian Perkins assumed that an authority higher than the crown was the source of authority for conscience. A brief survey of the emergence of these two attitudes will reveal more fully the difference between them.

A. *The Elizabethan Government and the Problem of Conscience*

In essence, the Elizabethan governmental attitude toward conscience was one of toleration, the notion of governmental toleration being a tradition. That toleration was a familiar idea in English politics before the accession of Elizabeth is not difficult to demonstrate, but an appreciation of that tradition depends, in some measure, upon an understanding of what is meant by the word *toleration*.

Toleration must be distinguished from *tolerance*. *Tolerance* means to possess a fair and objective attitude toward those whose opinions, practices, race, religion, or nationality differ from one's own; it is a freedom from bigotry. The key to the meaning of *tolerance* is its reference to a cast of mind; thus, *fair* or *objective*, indeed, the phrase, "an open mind," indicates the root meaning of the word. Though *tolerance* and *toleration* have the same Latin root (*tolero*), the word *toleration* has a narrower meaning. Most often it refers to legal situations in which a government *allows* a practice to continue even though the practice is not consistent with the established one. *Toleration* may, thus, be simply a refraining from persecution.

Toleration as descriptive of a governmental policy, according to one student of the problem, implies a "latent disapproval," a "limited and conditional freedom," and "an authority which has been and which again may become coercive."[5] From a different angle, "it implies . . . voluntary inaction on the part of the dominant group."[6] The heart of the idea of toleration has been succinctly stated:

> . . . [it] may be said to spring from the theory that the civil power has inalienable and absolute prerogatives. The Government thus elevated may allow certain persons to differ from it in theory and religious practice.[7]

An important point to grasp in comparing *tolerance* and *toleration* is the absence of any sense of objectivity and open-mindedness in the meaning of *toleration*. A government pursues a policy of toleration for reasons of state which are most often expedient reasons.[8] A second point that needs to be stressed is the implication in *toleration* that the state merely grants as a privilege what it tolerates, a grant that may be withdrawn.

The notion of toleration as a governmental grant was evident in early sixteenth-century England. Thomas More in his *Utopia* pictured King Utopus as following a policy of toleration:

> . . . [He] *gave* to every man liberty and choice to believe what he would. Saving that he earnestly and straightly charged them, that no man should conceive so vile and base an opinion of the dignity of man's nature, as to think that the soul do die and perish with the body; or that the world runneth at all adventures, governed by no divine providence.[9]

More here assumes that it was the king's prerogative to give what liberty he wished his subjects to have, and, importantly, he told them about two opinions he would not tolerate.

More's fictional king was more tolerant than his real one. More lived and wrote during the reign of Henry VIII, and Henry had something to say about what he would allow and what would not be tolerated. In 1536 he authorized the publication of "Articles about Religion," which includes the following description of Henry's view of his prerogatives:

> Amongst other cures committed unto our princely office . . . we have always esteemed and thought (as yet we esteem and think)

this to be most chief, most ponderous, and of most weight, that his [God's] holy word and commandments may sincerely without let or hindrance, be of our subjects truly believed, and reverently kept and observed. . . .[10]

Assuming as he did that it was a prerogative of his office as king to care for the religion of his subjects, Henry went on to say that "unity and concord in opinions, namely in such things as doth concern our religion" should increase. What Henry had to say about how "unity and concord" should be achieved reflects one form that a policy of toleration can take. In Henry's thinking, religion could be reverently kept and observed if "all occasion of dissent and discord touching the same be repressed, and utterly extinguished."[11]

More's description of King Utopus and Henry's "Articles about Religion" both reflect attitudes toward toleration; both assume that the king had the authority to care for religious affairs within the realm. Henry's wish that dissent be repressed appears to be substantially different from Utopus' two stipulations about death of the soul and divine providence. That Henry's Articles allowed his subjects less latitude than Utopus' stipulations does not materially change the fact that both policies rested upon the assumption that the king had the authority to grant toleration in whatever form he desired. To paraphrase Justice Oliver Wendell Holmes, either policy of toleration would be an insult to mankind, for toleration in any form is still toleration.[12]

Queen Elizabeth was heir to this policy of toleration, and she used it creatively as she consolidated her power after accession. One innovation made by Elizabeth and her government in the policy of toleration involved the problem of conscience, but how conscience was tolerated and what it meant must be seen in light of the terms and conditions that attended Elizabeth's accession.

The circumstances surrounding her accession were complex; extant evidence dating from that period is thin, but what the major issues were may be stated with some confidence.[13] For a decade before the accession of Elizabeth, England was in the process of deciding whether it would follow the Protestant Reformation or continue a modified Catholicism. Henry had set the tone for English

Reformation along the lines of a modified Catholicism. Under Edward VI events seemed to move in the direction of a Genevan Calvinism, but these developments suffered a relapse with the appearance of Mary Tudor. As Elizabeth came to power, the question as to whether England would follow Rome or Geneva was not settled. One issue, perhaps the most important one, as Elizabeth came to power was, therefore, the religious question.

How this question was answered may be seen in what historians call the Elizabethan Settlement.[14] Usually this phrase refers to a pair of Parliamentary bills passed during the first months of Elizabeth's reign, one called the Act of Supremacy, and the other, the Oath of Allegiance. The Settlement included these measures, but other factors were equally important. The bills themselves differed little from similar ones enacted during the rule of Henry and Edward, the one significant exception being the fact that Elizabeth was governor of the English Church instead of "supreme head" as Henry had been.[15]

Other elements in the Settlement included Elizabeth's decision and determination that England would be Protestant rather than Catholic, and the concomitant question of how English Catholics would be treated. The Catholic question, more than any other, reveals the way Elizabeth related the policy of toleration to the problem of conscience.

In essence, her position was that Catholics who objected to the legal requirements of the Settlement as injurious to conscience would be tolerated. That Elizabeth could consent to such a policy was, indeed, an innovation in light of Henry's desire that "unity and concord" be achieved through repression of dissent. Whether Elizabeth had great personal respect for conscience is not clear from existing records, but her private views are not important, nor critical, for an understanding of how she could tolerate dissenting Catholic consciences.

The practical working out of the Settlement depended upon the personality and temperament of the queen.[16] She was no zealot religiously, despite the fact that she was determined that England be Protestant; thus, she could entertain reforms suggested by radical Puritans as well as those proffered by more moderate divines. Radical

Puritans desired the repression of Catholics, and of all evidence of Catholicism in the English Church, but the maneuverings by the Crown and its advisors as the Settlement bills were being drafted indicated Elizabeth's distaste for such measures.[17] She was willing to settle for a compromise between the demands of Puritans and Catholics.

The absence of religious zeal in Elizabeth was undoubtedly related to her political goals. Apparently she was determined that peace prevail on the domestic scene. If peace was to be achieved, religious interests would have to be subordinated to political ends. Accommodation of conflicting religious claims could be accomplished through tolearation. The essence of this arrangement has been described by one student of this period in these words:

> The Settlement of Religion was essentially political and national in character. . . . The doctrine set forth . . . was, in essence, that conscience was free, although the public exercise of any but the established religion was not to be tolerated.[18]

The first ten years of Elizabeth's reign appeared to confirm the wisdom of tolerating private deviation from public established religion, for during that time the religious scene was relatively calm.[19] By the end of the decade, however, the government found itself in the middle of a crisis, and that crisis revealed the emergence of conscience as a significant feature of the policy of toleration.

As a practical matter private religion was not greatly disturbed during the first decade even though many Catholics had refused to follow the legal requirements of the Settlement. By 1570, however, Rome decided to support actively Jesuit efforts toward conversion of England, and Mary Stuart's arrival in England provided a rallying point for any Catholics who entertained thoughts of returning England to Catholicism.[20] If these factors were not enough to disturb what might be called an equilibrium, Rome made matters worse by issuing the Bull *Regnans in Excelsis,* which excommunicated the queen and absolved her subjects "from their oath of allegiance, and every other thing due unto her whatsoever."[21] The government had no choice but to scrutinize Catholic activities more closely.

The manner in which the government proceeded against Catholics had an important effect upon the role of conscience in the Elizabethan mind. Closer government scrutiny of religious practices evoked cries of persecution of conscience, and claims, like those noted above, that conscience "was not in the power of the greatest monarchy in the world."[22] The government's counter-claim that it had no intention of "molesting consciences in the cause of religion" could be regarded with cynicism, but there is ample evidence that it made an effort to avoid afflicting consciences for religious opinions. Consistent with the queen's view that religion was merely an aspect of politics, the government attempted to separate the question of political loyalty from religious opinion. This policy was enunciated by Cecil, one of the queen's leading ministers:

> There shall be no color or occasion given to shed the blood of any of her majesty's subjects that shall only profess devotion in their religion without bending their labors maliciously to disturb the (common) quiet of the realm, and therewith to cause sedition and rebellion to occupy the place of peace against it.[23]

The queen herself outlined her policy toward the Catholic threat in the document *Declaration of the Queen's Proceedings*.[24] She outlined the causes of the crisis and especially emphasized the element of foreign influences. A comparison of government under her direction with that of her predecessors would indicate, she argued, the benevolent conditions she had fostered. It was not her intention, she said, to persecute subjects for "matters of ceremonies," or any other outward functions of religion," as long as they shall in their outward conversation show themselves quiet and comfortable."[25] Emphasizing the distinction between political loyalty and religious opinion, the queen asserted that loyal subjects . . .

> shall certainly and quietly have and enjoy the fruits of our former accustomed favor . . . without any molestation to them by any person by way of examination or inquisition of their secret opinions in their *consciences*, for matters of faith.[26]

Elizabethan governmental attitudes toward conscience emerged in the context of the traditional policy of toleration. Elizabeth's determination that England be Protestant naturally raised the question of how to deal with Catholics who could not in good conscience follow all the legal requirements of the Settlement of Religion. The queen and the government were willing to tolerate Catholic objections to the Settlement that were rooted in conscience. Even after Catholicism appeared to present a more severe threat to political stability, the queen continued to tolerate tender Catholic consciences, provided, however, that political loyalty was assured.

B. *Elizabethan Puritans and the Problem of Conscience*

The government's disposition to tolerate Catholic consciences as a matter of political policy had an unexpected side effect, that is, an increasing number of Protestant dissenters defended their position in the name of conscience. Though minor dissenting groups were involved in such appeals, the most significant group was the party known as Puritans.[27]

The first puritan, who he was, and the last one, who he will be, no one knows, for the term properly applies to any and all who share a spirit of piety and concern for purity in the Christian life. Historic Puritanism, however, as a distinct movement began in the English Church during the reign of Elizabeth I.[28] It was a movement aimed at improving the quality of spiritual life in the English Church, but it was no mystical quietism concerned with an elusive and subjective inner life.[29] Puritan piety involved the question of the inner life, but its standard was the Bible, and Puritans viewed the Bible as an authoritative and infallible guide. Conventional English churchmen, without a doubt, could assent to the same view of the Holy Word, but they were content to follow tradition and place confidence in conciliar and confessional interpretations of what it was that Scriptures meant.[30] These churchmen, thus, held a view of the Bible that was consistent with the assumption of the government's role in policing religious practice, including the policy of toleration.

The supremacy and infallibility of the Scriptures as rule and guide for the Puritan was linked to another distinctive assumption, namely, the religious significance of the individual. Emphasis upon the supremacy of the Bible was inherited from Continental Reformers, such as Calvin, and from them the English Puritans learned to appreciate the idea of the priesthood of all believers.[31] In this view the individual was finally responsible for the condition of his soul as it progressed in the sanctified life. No priest or church or government could act or believe, or refrain from acting or believing, for him. The Puritan as a Reformed Christian, as a believer in the supremacy of the Scriptures, as a believer in the significance of the individual, was confronted with the question of how it was that he stood alone before God and His revelation in the Scriptures. His answer was quite simple: God as creator had endowed him with a conscience, and it was through his conscience that he knew how to act or believe, or how not to act or not to believe.

Puritan theologians developed a description of the morphology of conscience that was consistent with their general theory of knowledge, and in due course that argument will be examined,[32] but first something more needs to be said about the Puritan view of conscience during the first years of the Age of Elizabeth.

Puritanism as a distinct movement began in Cambridge University, and it is significant, therefore, that Puritans in Cambridge as early as 1564 defended themselves in the name of conscience. Elizabethan governmental policy had established the Ecclesiastical Commission, whose purpose was to enforce the Acts of Uniformity.[33] Uniformity called for wearing of vestments by preachers, a practice that some Cambridgemen had neglected. They were called before the Commission, and there they justified their failure to wear them in the name of conscience. Wearing vestments was against their conscience; and "conscience was a tender thing, that ought not to be touched or angered," they said.[34]

These Cambridgemen were especially concerned about the question of vestments because vestments were a matter indifferent. In speaking of indifferent matters the Cambridge preachers referred to practices that had no scriptural rule. Religious practices that had no definite scriptural basis were especially important to them because in such things each person had liberty to suit his own taste, this being the Christian liberty that St. Paul had so often talked about.[35]

The Cambridge preachers argued that they agreed with the teaching of the English Church in fundamental doctrines, but that vestments were not a question of fundamentals. In the Puritan view the commission did not have the authority, therefore, to meddle in this question. Their final appeal before the Commission stated that "they were taught by conscience, that things in their own nature indifferent do not always seem indifferent to the opinions of men, and are changed by times and accidents."[36]

Some Cambridgemen were disturbed enough to complain to Cecil. In their protest to him they stated that "slavery of the body is grievous, but that of the mind, tormented with daily racks of the conscience, is more sharp than the most exquisite torments."[37] One preacher petitioned the queen herself on the vestment issue, and his stand was that "liberty of conscience ought by no means to be restrained."[38]

Puritan appeals to conscience in the early years of the Elizabethan Age were tolerated by the government. Lord Burleigh, another of the queen's advisors, in commenting on the fact that "good preachers" had been indicted for "swerving from the letter of the law," suggested to the Justices of the Peace that they try to relieve the pressure of indictment against these men.[39] Burleigh advised that if they had to proceed with the cases against the good preachers, the men not be treated as rogues or papists, rather that much be made of the difference between the papists "dissenting from us in substance of faith to God and loyalty to our prince, and these other men. . . ."[40] The other men, Puritan preachers, he said, make "some conscience in these ceremonies, [and] do yet diligently and soundly preach true religion and obedience to her majesty."[41]

On another occasion when the Church, under the leadership of Witgift, sought to suppress disloyal Catholics by tightening the bands of uniformity, Burleigh came to the aid of two harried Puritan preachers. Burleigh protested to Witgift that Witgift's techniques were in the "Romish style" and were used without distinction of person in examining ministers. Burleigh thought the techniques were so complicated that "the Inquisition of Spain used not so many questions to comprehend and trap their prey."[42] He saw no place for such theological formulation among "mere ministers," adding that such "does not edify and reform." In speaking of the Puritan preachers, Burleigh stated, "I think they ought not to answer to all these nice points."[43]

Puritan preachers, thus, defended themselves and their objection to certain religious practices by appealing to the rights of conscience, and these appeals were met with understanding by governmental officials. The Puritan practice of appealing to the rights of conscience in concrete circumstances continued throughout the Age of Elizabeth. Such appeals to conscience were more than expedient arguments, for conscience was increasingly understood as an integral part of Puritan theology.

To say that conscience became more of an integral aspect of Puritan theology requires some evaluation of what Puritan theology was. Puritanism as a movement and Puritan theology as an expression of that movement in the Age of Elizabeth did not appear as a monolithic, unified system.[44] This fact would seem to preclude reference to representative expressions of the Puritan mind during this time. Although new social and intellectual movements at times result from the efforts of a single individual, as in the case of Calvinism, more often they emerge as the product of what might be called a composite mind. Professor Haller in his searching studies of Puritanism has suggested that Elizabethan Puritanism was in essence the result of this type of phenomenon.[45] He identified the locus of Puritan thought in Cambridge University among what he called the Puritan brotherhood. What these men had to say about particular theological problems may be taken as representative of Puritan theology.

According to Haller, early Cambridge Puritanism centered around the leadership of Richard Rogers, Richard Greenham, John Dod, Arthur Hildersam, and Lawrence Chaderton.[46] What these men had to say about conscience, therefore, is important.

The Cambridge brotherhood's main concern was with the problem of the quality of spiritual life, with the question of the relationship between grace and works. As a practical theological issue the brotherhood saw the problem of grace and works as a question of the relationship between the Old Testament and the New, between the demands of the law in the Old and the freedom taught in the New.

Characteristically John Dod wrote about the Ten Commandments, stating their sole purpose to be "to stir us up . . . in conscience."[47] He viewed the Commandments as a "preparation" and not an end in themselves, nor as a "yoke or bondage."[48] Dod's colleague, Richard Rogers, had the same attitude toward the law of the Old Testament; he wrote, "Law is not preached to hold men under, with the yoke of fear and bondage . . . but to set more stores by God's mercy."[49]

It is fair to say that the brotherhood viewed conscience as a means of grace, as a bridge between the demands of the old law and the freedom taught in the gospel. As noted, Dod wrote that the purpose of the law was to stir men up in conscience; Rogers thought it essential to "get and keep a good conscience." Hildersam saw conscience as "a device that either keeps a heart in joy or sorrow," basing his comment upon St. Paul's statement, "For our rejoicing is this, the testimony of a good conscience."[50]

Another of the brotherhood, Richard Greenham, had more to say about conscience. As to what it was, he wrote, "Conscience is a sensible feeling of God's judgments grounded upon the Word, nourished by the consideration of the last day, stirring up our hearts to the approving of our doings both before God and man."[51] Greenham metaphorically described the sense of freedom he felt conscience had in these words:

> We must not make our conscience like a chesverel [kid-leather purse], stretch it too far, or too narrow, that is, be not too righteous, as the Anabaptists, and the Family of love. . . . We must not let our conscience be looser than the Scripture be, for then we shall be prophane. Take heed of extremes, for virtue is a mean between extremes, taking something of one, and something of the other: knowledge of generals and conscience of particulars.[52]

In Greenham's view, conscience was a capacity in man that allowed him to bridge the gap between moral demands of Scripture and particular actions. Moreover, it had an elasticity and latitude—not to be stretched too far, nor too little.

Mention of conscience by early Cambridge Puritans suggests that it was part of their theological baggage, but not a particularly important part. For some, it was a means of grace that softened the demands of Old Testament law. That conscience had latitude and liberty, in their view, seems evident in the writing of Greenham. These early Cambridge Puritans did not, as might be suspected, feel any compulsion to write a systematic treatise on conscience and its problems. That task was taken up by a younger member of the brotherhood, William Perkins.

C. *William Perkins: A Theology of Conscience*

William Perkins came to Cambridge University in 1577, and found the atmosphere there already charged with a zeal aimed at upgrading the quality of spiritual life in the English Church and in society. Like many of his contemporaries, Perkins experienced a dramatic conversion, and thereafter vigorously pursued a life of piety.[53] Perkins was a gifted preacher and writer, gaining a reputation early in his career. Though he died in 1602 at the age of forty-four, he left behind three large tomes of theological tracts and treatises. From the standpoint of sheer production, Perkins wrote more than any other Elizabethan Puritan.

Perkins' writings differ in an important way from those of his contemporaries, for they evidence an intense interest in conscience not found in the works of his Puritan peers. In fact, it may be argued that Perkins' emphasis on conscience was the foundation of a new theology, one that may be labeled a "theology of conscience."[54] To suggest that Perkins created a new theology does not mean that standard Puritan theological doctrines were cast aside. Puritan theological mainstays, such as the sovereignty of God, justification by faith, and other traditional Reformed doctrines, were retained by Perkins, but were viewed in light of their relationship to conscience.

The root of Perkins' theology of conscience was the assumption that conscience played a vital role in determining the condition of the soul. Christians have always been interested in, and, indeed, concerned for, the condition of the soul, but Perkins taught that conscience was the means or device that allowed Christians to determine with a high degree of accuracy the condition of the soul. His emphasis on conscience forced him to define it and describe how it worked. This he did in a number of treatises on conscience itself and in other works that were descriptive of how conscience operated.[55] Perkins' basic treatise on conscience was called the *Discourse*.[56] This work, coupled with his "Cases on Conscience," defines conscience and outlines the basic types of problems of conscience. That conscience comprehended the whole of theological speculation for Perkins may be appreciated from the fact that he described the problem of salvation itself as "the case of conscience, the greatest that ever was."[57]

Though Perkins' role in the creation of a theology of conscience needs to be better known[58] comment here will be restricted to an examination of his definition of conscience and its effect upon the Elizabethan interest in liberty of conscience.

Perkins' definition of conscience embraced two important assumptions—the authority of Scripture and faculty psychology—and these account for his unique definition of conscience. Exaggeration of one or the other of these elements distorts Perkins' definition.

The assumption of scriptural authority affected Perkins' view of conscience in two ways. First, Perkins found in the New Testament explicit warrant for the doctrine of conscience. St. Paul was the chief expounder of the idea of conscience, and often mentioned the freedom and liberty that the Christian had by way of conscience.[59] Perkins' theology of conscience was an elaboration of the Pauline principle. Following St. Paul, Perkins argued that the Christian conscience was always regulated normatively by the Bible, particularly the New Testament. As he described the duties of conscience and its liberty, he always did so in light of biblical teachings. From the standpoint of the internecine dispute among Elizabethans about the source of authority, Perkins' theological stance reinforced the Puritan claim that biblical authority transcended that of the state.[60]

Describing conscience in terms of the faculty psychology was a second important feature of Perkins' theology of conscience. Use of faculty psychology was, of course, not an innovation on Perkins' part; rather, it was a conscious imitation of Roman Catholic writers.[61] According to faculty psychology, conscience was part of the understanding, understanding being one of two parts of the soul, the will being the other. Conscience was linked to the understanding because its operation involved reason; reason was an essential factor in understanding. Perkins illustrated his contention that conscience was part of the understanding by using the homely example of the "wagoner and the wagon." As the wagoner guides the wagon, so, too, reason and conscience in the understanding guide man. Will, by contrast, only has the power to choose or refuse some course of action; it can give no direction.[62]

Perkins made a further division, separating understanding into the theoretical and practical. Theoretical understanding judges truth and falsehood, but only in a contemplative way. Practical understanding, on the other hand, judges particular actions, determining whether they are good or bad. Conscience, Perkins concluded, was part of the practical understanding, for its business was to judge specific actions.[63]

Further distinctions had to be made, according to Perkins, for conscience was not mere knowledge. If it were mere knowledge, it would be capable of being extinguished, and that is not possible, says Perkins. Conscience is a natural power, that is, a function of understanding, not a product of understanding as mere knowledge is. Perkins' claim that conscience was a natural power was based upon his own experience; he could in no way make conscience go away. This view also had support in St. Paul's letter to the Romans, wherein Paul taught that conscience might be perverted, but was always there as a testimony of God's law.[64]

Perkins' definition of conscience in terms of faculty psychology is not easy to comprehend, but his discussion of the purpose of conscience helps to bridge the gap between faculty psychology and the modern mind. Conscience, says Perkins, judges the actions of the person in whom it resides, giving approbation or condemnation.[65] Conscience functions only in relation to actions of the self of which it is a part, and thus cannot judge actions of other persons. That sense of right or wrong that one can have about the actions of others is for Perkins mere knowledge.[66]

An essential feature of conscience in Perkins' view is its testimonial character. By testimonial, Perkins means conscience's ability to speak to the rest of the self; herein he describes what others call "the voice of conscience."[67] Conscience testifies or witnesses to the rest of the self not only, but also to God. That conscience stands to witness to the self and to God is a fundamental point in Perkins' view. Conscience was placed in man by God, says Perkins, so that man would have a way to know whether his actions were consistent with God's moral law, or against it. In Perkins' words,

> Conscience is of a Divine nature, and is a thing placed of God in the middle between Him and man, as an arbitrator to give sentence, and to pronounce either with man or against man unto God.[68]

Perkins would admit that conscience had some sort of *a priori* sense of right and wrong, but that was not the source of information for a Christian conscience; the Christian informed his conscience by looking into the Bible, particularly at the moral law.[69] The moral law for Perkins was, however, more than the Decalogue of the Old Testament; it embraced the moral law taught in the New Testament as well.[70] How one applied the moral law was illustrated in his practical divinity or cases of conscience.

Two general characteristics of practical divinity help to keep it in perspective, help to define it for the modern mind. For Perkins, the sense of the moral law as taught in the Old Testament was always tempered by the freedom the Christian had in Christ. As a matter of fact, one may test the emphasis that a given Puritan placed on conscience by noting the weight that he gave to the New Testament over the Old. As will be evident, some Puritans stressed the Old to such an extent that they saw no particular value in the concept of conscience.[71] A second characteristic of practical divinity evident in Perkins and later Puritans was the disposition to align problems of conscience according to Christ's summary of the law. Thus, problems of conscience were one of three basic kinds—those between self and God, those between self and another person, or those involving only the self.[72] Within each of these general categories there was a place for every conceivable kind of problem, and they were organized by Perkins with an admirable display of logic.

The comprehensive nature of the general *schema* permitted, indeed, challenged, the commentator on practical divinity to write on every type of human relationship, including relationships among the church, state, and individuals. This class of problems appears to have been of special interest to Perkins; at least he deals with them at length and with force and conviction.[73] In the introduction to comments on the church and state, Perkins states the reason for treating the subject thoroughly, the belief that the Church of Rome had for so long distorted the role of conscience in the affairs of men. In his words,

> I will stand a while to examine and *confute* the opinion, that the very pillars of the popish church at this day maintain; namely, that civil and ecclesiastical jurisdiction have a coactive power in the conscience, and that the laws made thereby do as truly and properly bind as they speak to mortal and venial sin, as God's law itself.[74]

Perkins' concern for the practices of the Roman Church stems from the fact that, in his view, it had made great inroads on the liberty of conscience that naturally falls to the Christian man. It is important to note that he points out the two areas in which he feels Roman practice to have been detrimental, namely, in the church and in the state.

Concerning the church, Perkins says all those practices in the Roman tradition that do not have scriptural warrant are an unnecessary and unlawful intrusion upon the freedom and liberty of conscience taught in the New Testament.[75] In good Puritan style Perkins listed fourteen errors by way of illustration of his argument, refuting each in turn. One may serve adequately as an example. The fifth chapter of Galatians reads in part, "Stand ye in the liberty wherewith Christ hath freed you, and be not entangled with the yoke of bondage."[76] The meaning of this is clear to Perkins:

> God hath now in the new testament given a liberty to the conscience, whereby it is freed from all laws of his own whatsoever, excepting such laws and doctrines as are necessary to salvation.[77]

Perkins quotes an unnamed Roman author who states that this passage intends only to free men from the bondage of sin, from the curse of the moral law, and not from the laws of any superiors. Refuting this argument Perkins states,

> I answer again, that it is absurd to think that God gives us liberty in conscience from any of his own laws, and yet will have our consciences still remain in subjection to the laws of sinful men.[78]

This comment by Perkins not only reinforces his claim that man has liberty in the gospel, but significantly it suggests that man is not under *any* laws of other men. He is not, of course, preaching anarchy; rather he is emphasizing the fact that all laws come from God. This argument, found elsewhere in his writings, conflicts sharply with the assumption, noted earlier, of Elizabethan governmental officials, that the state had inherent power and authority. Christian men obey the state because obedience is required of them in the New Testament, not because of any inherent authority in the state, according to Perkins.[79] How it was that men obeyed the state, Perkins outlined in the same discussion of Roman errors.

Rome erred in teaching total subjection to civil authority as it did in teaching unscriptural obedience to the church. Thereafter Perkins outlined the manner in which one ought to relate to the state.[80] Some positive civil laws must be obeyed because they simply repeat moral laws of God, such as a law against murder. A second class of positive laws derive from the power that God has given to the magistrate for maintaining peace and the common good. These laws are called "wholesome laws" by Perkins,[81] but he does not intend this to be an open-ended category, or a *carte blanche* to magistrates. They consist of matters that are "indifferent," that is, matters that are not expressly commanded by God, and matters that do not fall within the bounds of liberty of conscience, such as paying taxes.[82]

Perkins mentions a third and rather interesting class of laws in civil matters; he calls them "penal." By this he means laws that are geared to regulation of such practices as commerce, or laws that are not clear in their intent, or laws that are not expressly commands. In all such matters, states Perkins, man is at liberty to do what he pleases as long as he is willing to suffer the punishment if charged.[83] Clearly in civil affairs, Perkins is not one of those who teach that a law is a law, and therefore must be obeyed in every and all circumstances.

Perkins' description of how the individual relates to the power of the state was not only unconventional in terms of the prevailing views in Elizabethan society, it had revolutionary implications. It may be granted that in operation Perkins' Christian man obeyed most of the laws that others obeyed; he did not murder, nor did he steal. The critical and fundamental difference between Perkins' view and that of others focused in a small area, but that did not diminish the significance of the fact that Perkins' system rested upon a different concept of power and authority.

Perkins' system may best be described as sphere sovereignty, a phrase sometimes used to describe Calvin's view of institutions.[84] The phrase posits the assumption that all institutions have as their source of authority the creation ordinances of God. Each institution was created for a purpose, and therefore was given certain powers and a specific jurisdiction. What these features were could be known by an examination of the order implicit in the creation, and by written revelation in the Bible.[85] Basic institutions included family, church, state, and industry, each standing side by side under the all-encompassing sovereignty of God. Without man, of course, none of these institutions existed; hence, the idea results that institutions exist to serve man. Man, too, relates directly and primarily to God. This is what Perkins had in mind when he objected to the Roman view that civil and ecclesiastical jurisdictions have a coactive power in the conscience, and that laws made by these institutions had an effect equal to "God's law itself." In sphere sovereignty and in Perkins' view, man obeys the state, or church, because he has a divine injunction to obey in those cases in which the state or church has jurisdiction. That he obeys the law of the state is coincidental to the fact that he is obeying God first.

Only when Perkins' view of authority is appreciated for its radical departure from prevailing views, can his comments on the individual's opposition to the laws of the state be grasped. Maladministration by lesser magistrates did not appear to pose a serious problem for Perkins; it may be surmised that he advocated redress by appeal to a higher magistrate.[86] If the state over-reached its authority in fundamental questions, such as in matters of religion, Perkins' Christian man had to be civilly disobedient:

> If it should fall out that men's laws be made of things evil, and forbidden by God, then there is no bond of conscience at all: but contrariwise men are bound in conscience not to obey.[87]

That men are bound in certain instances not to obey governmental demands was no Perkinsian whim, it striking the same chord that appears in Calvin. Calvin's language is a bit stronger; he argues that rather than obey a law that is contrary to God's moral law, the Christian subject ought rather to "spit in the face of the magistrate."[88] The point is the same, however, for both teach that man owes obedience to God first.

Perkins' contribution to the development of an understanding of liberty of conscience was monumental though his contribution has not been fully appreciated. Perhaps his most significant achievement was a systematic definition of what conscience was in the Christian and Reformed perspective. His view of conscience as a reliable and reasonable device standing as an authoritative witness to man and God pervaded Reformed thinking for the following two centuries.[89] Important, too, was his systematic description of how conscience worked with regard to specific problems, such as church-state relations.

Liberty of conscience was a fundamental aspect of Perkins' whole concept of conscience, and it was used in several ways. His statement that "God hath now in the new testament given a liberty to the conscience" reflects his general view of liberty of conscience. This statement does not imply license or anarchy, nor does it suggest that man is a totally free and autonomous spirit. The Christian man is bound to obey scriptural injunctions, and what these were Perkins outlined in his practical divinity. Concerning religion, the Christian was bound to obey the basic doctrines of salvation. In Perkins' view the Apostles' Creed would probably be an adequate summary, though the Bible was the final test of what was essential.

Perkins' description of how the Christian ought to relate to the state shows another aspect of his view of liberty of conscience.

As in religion, certain basic duties were encumbent if some semblance of order was to be maintained, but Perkins would not allow all laws in the name of order. Laws aimed at regulation of commerce, for example, did not bind the conscience. In such matters, thus, man had liberty of conscience to pursue his own goals.

More serious, however, was the question of laws that conflicted with the moral laws of God. In such cases the Christian's liberty of conscience was not circumscribed by the demands of the state. This point is best understood in terms of the idea of sphere sovereignty. The church, the state, and man have their areas of duty and authority, but the source of authority in each case is not in one for the other; rather all have their authority first of all from God. The implications of this view for liberty of conscience suggest that man is at liberty in relation to the other spheres, submitting to them only as there is scriptural warrant. For Perkins, then, the assumption is that man has liberty of conscience in relation to the state except in those matters in which he is bound by Scripture to obey.

In summary, William Perkins was an important figure in the development of the concept of liberty of conscience, and for several reasons. His systematic definition of conscience in terms of Scripture and faculty psychology was normative for generations to come. In addition, his definition of conscience within this framework provided a working definition of what that liberty was that "God hath now in the new testament given" to conscience. No doubt Perkins' Christian man had many duties to the church, state, and other men; but beginning as he does with the view that the New Testament Christian has liberty of conscience, his position differs radically from that of Queen Elizabeth and her government.

As the Age of Elizabeth came to a close, it was clear that two distinct attitudes toward conscience had developed. One, fostered by governmental officials and others who supported traditional patterns of English thought, viewed conscience as a practice within the purview of governmental authority. In terms of sphere sovereignty this meant the government assumed that all matters of conscience came within its jurisdiction. While the government assumed full jurisdiction over individual consciences, there were always matters of conscience that it could concede to its subjects. Those matters it chose to concede constituted its policy of toleration.

A second attitude toward conscience developed in the Puritan community, its chief spokesman being William Perkins. It posited conscience as a faculty of man that transcended all other forms of authority. Conscience stood above the authority of men and institutions because it was immediately subject to God. While conscience was bound in certain cases, it was bound only in those instances clearly spelled out in God's Word. In terms of sphere sovereignty, conscience stood apart from the jurisdictions of the state and church. In other words, the conscience of the individual was at liberty, was a sphere by itself.

These two views—toleration and liberty of conscience—continued in Old England as the seventeenth century opened. During the first four decades they were more frequently a factor in political and religious affairs.

CHAPTER NOTES

1. William Cobbett, *The Parliamentary History of England* (London, 1806), I, p. 763.
2. *S.P., Dom. Elizabeth.*, LXXI, p. 16.
3. William Perkins, *Works* (London, 1612-1618), I, p. 529.
4. *S.P., Dom. Eliz.*, XVIII, p. 28.
5. Jordan, *Toleration*, I, p. 17.
6. *Ibid.*
7. *Ibid.*
8. For an excellent study of the development of state policy see George L. Mosse, *The Holy Pretence: A Study of Christianity and Reason of State from William Perkins to John Winthrop* (London, 1957).
9. Thomas More, *Utopia* (London, 1895), p. 529 (italics mine).
10. Thomas Burnet, *History of the Reformation* (London, 1865), I, p. 272.
11. *Ibid.*
12. Jordan, *Toleration*, I, pp. 17-18, quotes Holmes on toleration.
13. Although I have relied on Jordan's discussion of Elizabethan political events, J. E. Neale's study, *Elizabeth I and Her Parliaments 1559-1581* (London, 1958), is a more detailed study of the inside workings of the Elizabethan government. The discussion in this essay of the Elizabethan Settlement follows Neale's excellent account; hereafter cited as Neale, *Elizabeth*.

14. Neale, *Elizabeth*, chap. II.
15. *Ibid.*, p. 73; see also Jordan, *Toleration*, I, p. 84.
16. Neale, *Elizabeth*, pp. 117-121, 160-161, 230, 241, 311-312, 387-392, as well as chap. I; see also Jordan, *Toleration*, I, p. 111.
17. *Ibid.*, pp. 51-52.
18. Jordan, *Toleration*, I, p. 85.
19. *Ibid.*; compare pp. 99-111 with 112-131.
20. *Ibid.*, p. 112.
21. *Ibid.*, p. 118.
22. *Supra*, p. 4.
23. Jordan, *Toleration*, I, p. 120.
24. *Ibid.*, p. 121.
25. *Ibid.*, p. 125.
26. *Ibid.*, p. 126 (italics mine).
27. See Jordan, *Toleration*, I, pp. 261-299, for a discussion of these groups.
28. L. J. Trinterud's "The Origins of Puritanism," *Church History*, XX (1951), pp. 37-57, is a useful introduction to the problem.
29. Daniel B. Shea, Jr., *Spiritual Autobiography in Early America* (Princeton, 1968) may be mentioned as evidence of a new interest in the problem of Puritan spiritual or inner life. In certain points Norman Pettit's *The Heart Prepared* (New Haven, 1966) is also a comment on the inner life. How Puritan concern for the inner life was related to other manifestations of the same concern has not been studied; at least I have not seen such a study. Even a cursory knowledge of Quietism as evidenced in the works of Miguel de Molinos, for example, would suggest that the question of the nature of the inner life for the Christian man was a question common to many in the sixteenth and seventeenth centuries. For an introduction to the works of Molinos, see J. Bigelow's *Molinos the Quietist* (New York, 1882).
30. Neale, *Elizabeth*, p. 89 ff.
31. See my article, "The Appeal to Conscience," in *Christianity Today*, XXIII (May 23, 1969), pp. 6-8, for a brief description of this point.
32. See below, p. 17 ff., and see also Thomas Wood's *English Casuistical Divinity During the Seventeenth Century* (London, 1952), chap. II, on the "Court of Conscience."
33. Jordan, *Toleration*, I, p. 100, and Neale, *Elizabeth*, p. 191 ff.
34. Jordan, *Toleration*, I, pp. 252-253.
35. For a listing of St. Paul's references to Christian liberty, see C. A. Pierce, *Conscience in the New Testament* (London, 1958).
36. Jordan, *Toleration*, I, p. 253.
37. *Ibid.*
38. *Ibid.*
39. *Ibid.*, p. 178.
40. *Ibid.*
41. *Ibid.*
42. *Ibid.*, p. 180.

43. *Ibid.*
44. For a study that suggests an essential unity, see Charles and Katherine George, *The Protestant Mind of the English Reformation, 1570-1640* (Princeton, 1961).
45. William Haller, *The Rise of Puritanism* (New York, 1958), pp. 5-6; hereinafter cited as Haller, *Rise*. Perry Miller takes the same stance in his book, *The New England Mind*, I, in chapters III and IV. Carl Becker, *The Heavenly City of the Eighteenth-Century Philosophers* (New Haven, 1932), demonstrated more than any recent historians the value of the idea of composite thinking, or, as he called it, "Climates of Opinion."
46. Haller, *Rise*, chap. II.
47. John Dod, *A Plain and Familiar Explanation of the Ten Commandments* (London, 1609), p. 4.
48. *Ibid.*, p. 5.
49. Richard Rogers, *Seven Treatises* [Toward] *True Happiness* (London, 1610), p. 6.
50. Arthur Hildersam, *CVII Lectures on the Fourth of John* (London, 1642), pp. 396-397.
51. Richard Greenham, *Works* (London, 1620), pp. 816-817.
52. *Ibid.*
53. See *D.N.B.*, XLV, pp. 6-9; and J. T. McNeill's "Casuistry in the Puritan Age," *Religion and Life*, XII (1943), pp. 76-89.
54. See my essay referred to, *supra*, p. 11. As far as I know others have not used this phrase.
55. For Perkins' works that deal with conscience, see bibliography below.
56. The *Discourse* appears in his *Works*, I, pp. 515-554.
57. Perkins, *Works*, I, p. 421, "A Case of Conscience, The Greatest that ever was: how a man may know whether he be the child of God, or not."
58. As far as I know the only study of Perkins in the modern period is Ian Breward's Ph.D. thesis (1963), done in Manchester University. I have not been able to obtain a copy of this study, however.
59. See my article cited, *supra*, p. 11.
60. *Infra*, pp. 89-91, for a further discussion of this point in terms of sphere sovereignty.
61. See Thomas Wood, *English Casuistical Divinity* (London, 1952), chap. I, for a discussion of how Puritans used faculty psychology.
62. Perkins, *Works*, I, pp. 515-516.
63. *Ibid.*
64. See J. N. Sevenster, *Paul and Seneca* (Leiden, 1961), pp. 84-102, for a discussion of Paul's view of conscience.
65. Perkins, *Works*, I, p. 517.
66. *Ibid.*
67. This phrase is assumed to be a modern commonplace.

68. Perkins, *Works*, I, p. 517.
69. *Ibid.*, p. 518.
70. *Ibid.*
71. *Infra*, pp. 61-63.
72. Perkins, *Works*, I, p. 518
73. *Ibid.*, pp. 525-530.
74. *Ibid.*, p. 529 (italics mine).
75. *Ibid.*, p. 525.
76. Galatians 5:1.
77. Perkins, *Works*, I, p. 529.
78. *Ibid.*, p. 530.
79. *Ibid.*
80. *Ibid.*
81. *Ibid.*
82. *Ibid.*
83. *Ibid.*
84. Herman Dooyeweerd, *A New Critique of Theoretical Thought* (Philadelphia, 1958), IV, p. 221.
85. J. M. Spier, *An Introduction to Christian Philosophy* (Philadelphia, 1954), p. 31.
86. Perkins, *Works*, I, p. 530.
87. *Ibid.*
88. John Calvin, *Institutes* (Philadelphia, 1960), II, p. 1519, n. 54.
89. The problem of the demise of this view will be discussed in the concluding chapter of this essay.

Chapter II

TOLERATION AND LIBERTY OF CONSCIENCE IN OLD ENGLAND: 1600-1640

The division among Elizabethans as to the role of conscience in the affairs of men continued during the period 1600-1640, becoming a more prominent element in political and religious disputes. An appreciation of the significance of the continued division among Englishmen on the question of conscience requires an understanding of governmental policy concerning toleration, and a sense of the range and variety of people who came to embrace the idea of liberty of conscience during this period. One additional factor contributed to the division among Englishmen during this period, it being the doctrine of conscience enunciated by William Ames. Ames deserves special consideration in this period because of the influence he had upon subsequent developments in America.

A. *Toleration Under the Early Stuarts: 1600-1640.*

As the seventeenth century opened, the reign of Elizabeth came to a close. The great queen had presided over the laying of the foundation of Protestant England. An important feature of her domestic policy was its stance toward dissenters. She had demonstrated that a steady policy of toleration was a practical way to handle the tender consciences of her subjects. What the fortunes of this policy would be in the future depended in a large measure upon the character of her successors, the first being James I.

James was, in some ways, an unusual king, for he was a man of erudition, and a man with a facile pen. Before acceding to the English throne in the spring of 1603, James had written a number of treatises on government. In one of them he complained about the treatment accorded the Puritan preacher Cartwright, the latter having been imprisoned. Such treatment was a great slander, he wrote, considering "the great duty which we owe to such as are afflicted for their conscience in that profession." On another occasion he said that he had no quarrel with earnest men who disagreed with the Church on matters of form or ceremony.[1] James preferred that his subjects "content themselves soberly and quietly with their own opinions, not resisting to the authority, nor breaking the law of the country."[2] The last part of the statement was of course the nub of the matter. What James thought of disturbers of the peace and those who were not content to live quietly was evident in his opinion of the Dutch Arminians. To him they were "pestilent heretics," people "who dare take upon them that licentious liberty, to fetch from hell the ancient heresies long since condemned."[3]

The contrast between James' opinion of Cartwright and his description of the Dutch Arminians indicates an ambivalence in his thinking on the problem of toleration. He could appear noble and generous; at other times he sounded repressive. Throughout his career as king of England he vacillated from the one stance to the other, depending upon the nature of the immediate circumstances. One student of this period captured the essence of James's position when he wrote:

> James always expressed himself freely and enthusiastically in his written works and was invariably indignant when glaring discrepancies were pointed out between his theory and practice as King of England.[4]

James's noble rhetoric, written or spoken, did not alter the fact that his basic position on toleration was no different from that of Elizabeth. Like the great queen, he could order the execution of heretics, and do so as a matter of policy; yet he could press for a greater toleration of lay-Catholics. No doubt his temper was inclined toward less repressive measures, for he could say that no one ever became a Christian by coercion.[5] Retention of power, even the throne itself, however, dictated a less compassionate course on occasion.

In general, James's policy of toleration was moderate, but his disposition toward leniency in dealing with lay-Catholics was to have a profound effect on the fate of toleration under his son and successor, Charles I. During the first decade of his reign James spoke of his affection for loyal "spiritual Catholics," "spiritual" meaning laymen who were not associated with Jesuit plots to re-convert England.[6] This stance raised the ire of Protestants who always feared Rome and its real or imagined designs. James backed away from his embrace of lay-Catholics, but the need of a marriage partner for his son brought the Catholic problem to the fore again.[7]

The number of potential brides was limited; usually the possibilities were Catholic. As plans for Charles's future thus were made, they involved negotiations with a Catholic monarch. As early as 1614 serious discussions began with Spain in an attempt to procure a mate for Charles.[8] In this, and in subsequent negotiations with France,[9] the role of English Catholics seemed always to be an issue. Spain and France wanted to conclude a treaty which expressly stated that the rights of English Catholics would be protected. While there are many interesting facets to these negotiations, the most important in terms of the problem of toleration was the impact that these negotiations had on the English domestic scene.[10]

While James apparently wanted nothing more than a bride for his son, a substantial segment of English society believed that a Catholic princess, if not the treaty that would bring her to England, threatened Protestantism. Suspicion of the implications of a marriage treaty created a fissure between the more militant Protestants and traditional churchmen, a development that was to polarize religious factions.

Charles's actions upon accession in 1625 seemed to many Protestant members of Parliament a confirmation of their suspicion. Although there had been numerous factions within the English Church since the days of Elizabeth, the stance had been distinctly Reformed. Now, with the blessing of Charles, one of the minor factions was coming to dominate the shape of church policy. "Anglo-Catholic" best describes this group and its most famous spokesman, William Laud.[11]

Tomes have been written on the theology and policies of this party, and most of it has been written from a partisan point of view.

While Laud retained doctrines that were within the broad spectrum of Protestant thought, he favored policies that seemed to foster a closer association with Rome. Laud favored, for example, a streamlining of the chain of authority in the Church, with the Convocation at the top having final authority. Laud and his supporters warmly supported Charles, and he did not appear to discourage them, leading some to suppose that Charles actively supported Laud's program. As for dissenters, Laud encouraged a repressive policy toward them.[12]

Opposition to Laud and Anglo-Catholicism appeared early in Charles's reign, and it continued until the beginning of the Civil War. In fact, a central theme in English political and religious history from 1625 to the Civil War was the conflict between Charles and the Anglo-Catholic party, and Parliament under the leadership of Reformed Protestants.

The rise of Anglo-Catholicism under Charles altered the policy of toleration created by Elizabeth and followed, more or less, by James I. Earlier the success of the policy had depended upon its rather even application to both Catholic and Protestant dissenters. Now, however, it seemed to Protestants that the government and leading Church officials were disposed to treat Catholics warmly. This fear was not without foundation, as the activities of Charles and William Laud testify.

The more repressive attitude on the part of the Crown was linked to two persistent problems that Charles inherited: a tradition of parliamentary opposition to court policy, and a tangle of foreign affairs.[13] From the days of Elizabeth there had been a growing boldness on the part of Parliament when it came to the examination of government policies, the threat of the purse often held as a club to enforce parliamentary will. A shy man, and unpolitique, Charles was irritated when his requests for funds were denied or given only token support. The question of war and its prosecution accented the need for funds, and the question of the meaning of the war and its attendant alliances provoked suspicion among many in Parliament. In short, Charles's relationship to Parliament was uncomfortable at best, and in the long run proved unworkable.[14]

The suspicion and hostility in Parliament that was linked to

Charles's inability to present his programs for war was fueled further by the steady rise of William Laud and like-minded churchmen. Not only was Laud favored by Charles, the Catholic queen's friends seemed to gain in influence and power. Sympathy for Rome, both in the person of the queen and in the High Church views of Laud, ran as an undercurrent in the continuing debates between Charles and Parliament.

In the context of suspicion and hostility, and with sympathy for Rome as an undercurrent, more repressive measures on the part of the government were inevitable. Parliamentary leaders did not fail to notice the advance of harsher measures, and they indicated where it was they thought it would lead.

In the early days of Charles's first Parliament a debate commenced concerning the provisions of the marriage treaty.[15] Some members charged that Charles had broken the promises of his father, James, in that he accorded special privileges to Jesuits. Vigorous measures were demanded against Jesuits. Next, Parliament turned to an examination of a recently published book, *A New Gagg for an Old Goose*, written by Richard Montague.[16] This book was attacked because it was alleged to have dishonored the late King James and to have treated the rights of Parliament with contempt. More to the point was Montague's contention that the Puritans were worse than papists, fighting words to be sure. The Commons voted to send Montague to prison, and a committee was appointed to take up the matter with the king. The committee was informed that the king desired Montague to be set free. Shortly thereafter Montague was appointed royal chaplain.[17]

Following this incident, one in which Parliament felt itself again circumvented, parliamentary rhetoric became more vitriolic. Charles attempted to stem the flow of criticism by issuing a proclamation against religious dispute and by pleading for peace and unity, but his efforts were of no avail.[18] Parliament attacked Lord Buckingham, a long-time royal confidant, and protested against "the daily growth and spread of Arminianism," which they regarded as "but a cunning way to bring in popery."[19] By "Armininianism" Parliament meant the views of Laud and his party. One member spoke of Laud and his program as one in which "new paintings are laid on the old face of the whore Babylon [Rome], to make her show more lovely, and to draw so many suitors to her."[20] More specifically, the Commons had a duty:

> . . . to look into the very belly and bowels of the Trojan horse, to see if there be not men in it ready to open the gates to Romish tyranny, and Spanish monarchy; for an Arminian is the spawn of the papist.[21]

The consensus of Parliament by 1629 was that Charles and the Anglo-Catholic party would return the English Church to Rome. With this view in mind, and coupled with the fact that larger numbers of dissenters were harassed and imprisoned, Parliament had solid ground on which to contend that Englishmen were becoming the victims of a tyranny unknown since the days of Henry VIII.

The significance of the policy of toleration under the early Stuarts, particularly under Charles, is not so much that it continued a policy begun by Elizabeth; rather, it is in the fact that the policy became more repressive. As the government narrowed the limits of what it would allow in its policy of toleration, it drove more people into the camp of those who sought reform, of those who found in the idea of liberty of conscience an argument for freedom. The steady growth of affection for the cause of liberty of conscience apparently evaded the perception of Laud and King Charles, for as the shrewd Venetian ambassador observed:

> The King, seeing this poison spreading, tries to keep it far from his heart and to pull out its roots, but the more he tries to extirpate them the stronger they become.[22]

In 1629 Charles dissolved Parliament and ruled without parliamentary advice for more than a decade. The policy of toleration on the part of the government was enforced fitfully during the period 1629-1640, but the accession of William Laud to the archbishopric of Canterbury strengthened Laud's position to vex more vigorously dissenters and to imprison them.[23]

B. *A Wider Acceptance of Liberty of Conscience: 1600-1640*

Appeals to conscience grew at a rapid rate under the early Stuarts, such appeals emerging in virtually every segment of English society. To bring the range of opinions on conscience within manageable limits, and to account for the extraordinary interest in the notion of conscience, it will be useful to examine the variety of persons and groups in terms of two main categories. One category encompasses those persons that have been traditionally considered sectarian, while the other includes such persons as remained members, usually clergymen, of the English Church. The former category is composed of persons who were outspoken advocates of liberty of conscience; while the latter includes persons who aided the cause of liberty of conscience through the advocacy of complementary ideas and programs.

Historically much has been made of the differences between sectarian groups that emerged during the reign of Elizabeth and under the early Stuarts. Although students of the period cannot often agree on the unique features of particular groups, they are sure that evident differences are important. For example, among historians of Puritanism much energy has been spent in an attempt to determine how followers of John Robinson at Plymouth Colony differed from the builders of the Bay Colony of Massachusetts.[24] Were the Plymouth people separatists? Were the Massachusetts Bay colonists separatists? Equally important to students of this problem is the question as to the source of the idea of separatism.

Such arguments have tended to isolate the question of church polity—separate or congregational churches versus an established church—from other problems. The result has been that leaders of such groups have usually been viewed from the perspective of polity. Valuable though such a concern is, it has tended to obscure other questions about the thinking of these groups and their leaders. In a broad perspective it may be that the separatist tendencies of Robinson and others were more significant than any other aspects of their thought. It is a matter of judgment, but that issue should not be normative for what these men said about other issues.

With these observations in mind, it will be easier to appreciate the place of so-called separatists and congregationalists in the contest for liberty of conscience during the early Stuart era. Of course others have noted the fact that these groups spoke of liberty of conscience, but their pleas for liberty of conscience have been viewed as a function of their tendency toward separatism. William Bradshaw, John Smyth, Francis Johnson, and John Robinson have all been extolled as leaders of separatism, as fathers of congregationalism, or as founders of the Baptist movement. What has not been emphasized is the fact that these men were all part of the Cambridge community during the days of the Brotherhood, during the days of William Perkins. Concern for conscience and its liberty among these men is more likely a product of their consorting with other Puritans, such as Perkins, than their own creation in their struggles toward a separatist polity. Another feature of their thinking supports this notion, that being the fact that each of them consistently argued for sphere sovereignty, for the created autonomy of religious life.

The linking of conscience to sphere sovereignty occurred often in the writings of men like John Smyth. Smyth wrote that the prince must "leave the Christian religion free to every man's conscience." The prince's power and authority allowed him to "handle only civil transgressions, injuries, and wrongs of man against man, in murder, adultery, theft, etc. for Christ only is the King and Lawgiver of the Church and conscience."[25]

John Robinson, famous as the father of the Pilgrim settlement in America, held the same view of civil power and conscience, despite the fact that he wrote several tracts against other views held by Smyth and his followers. The value of Robinson's conviction lay in the even-tempered mood in which he expressed himself. Robinson wrote that the prince may constrain men toward outward acts, "but of religious actions the proper end is not civil society"; that only comes by "faith, and devotion in the heart of the doers."[26] Again, he wrote, the civil government has "no power against the laws, doctrine, and religion of Christ." God did not give authority over conscience to any man, wrote Robinson, for he kept that power in his own hands, so that he alone might bring them to a knowledge of faith.[27]

Other leaders of the movements spawned by Cambridge Puritans were also vigorous in their defense of liberty of conscience. Thomas Helwys, leader of a splinter group from Smyth's congregation, wrote lucidly on the question in 1611-12. The record is not clear whether Helwys attended Cambridge, but he expressed the Perkinsian view of the duties and powers of the magistrate as they relate to conscience and in terms that betray a familiarity with treatises on the subject. Helwys, in preparing to return to England from Holland, wrote *A Declaration of Faith of English People, Remaining at Amsterdam in Holland*.[28] Conscious of James I's interest in control of dissent, Helwys stated clearly what his group believed, and why. "Magistracy is a holy ordinance of God," he wrote, and every person ought to be subject to it "not for fear only, but for conscience sake." Kings were set up by God to punish wrongdoing, and hence, it is "a fearful sin to speak evil of them that are in dignity, and to despise government." Christians should pay taxes, hold office, and support lawful government. Government should not be obeyed, however, if it commanded evil actions, for the children of God are not bound "of conscience to obey in any thing that is unholy and not good."[29]

A year later Helwys wrote *A Short Declaration of the Mystery of Iniquity*[30] in which he had more to say on the same subject. Boldly, he wrote to James that he was "a mortal man," and thus had "no power over ye immortal souls of his subjects, to make laws and ordinances for them and to set spiritual lords over them." Helwys sensed the logic of his argument and added that if the ruler had authority to make spiritual laws, "he is an immortal God, and not a mortal man." Helwys' prescription to remedy the evils of the church was for James to withdraw his support from it. Emphasizing again his belief in sphere sovereignty, Helwys wrote that the Kingdom of God is not of this world, and "with this kingdom, our lord the king [James] hath nothing to do." The king was thus a layman in the church like other men.[31]

In his comments on Queen Mary, Helwys pointed out another flaw in James's assumption that he had power to grant what toleration he wished in matters of conscience. James, the defender of Protestantism, would not concede that Mary had had authority to persecute her Protestant subjects. Helwys saw the logical impasse when he wrote:

> As Queen Mary by her sword of justice had no power over her subjects' conscience . . . neither hath our Lord the king by that

sword of justice power over his subjects' consciences: for all earthly powers are one and the same in their several dominions.[32] James could not escape the conclusion that if his power was legitimate, so it was with Mary.

Of course, Helwys was politique enough to suggest that it was not James's fault that the whole matter had been confused, the blame lying with the bishops and others who sought power.[33] Helwys' declaration was an eloquent statement of the practical implications of the doctrine of liberty of conscience, one that represented an increasingly popular stance.

Two years after Helwys' second Declaration, another important tract appeared on the subject of liberty of conscience. It was entitled *Religious Peace: or, A Plea for Liberty of Conscience*, written by Leonard Busher. Not much is known about Busher, but the tract was widely circulated during the first half of the seventeenth century.[34] Busher's argument follows the pattern set out in Helwys' works and thus need not be reviewed in detail here. In the heat of the Civil War the tract was reprinted with an introduction addressed to Presbyterians.[35] One example of Busher's view of conscience stands out from the rest. In a paraphrase of the Golden Rule he wrote:

> As the king would not have his subjects take away his life, because he is contrary to them in religion; so let not the king take away the subjects' lives, because they are contrary to the king in religion. And as you would not that men should force you to a religion against your consciences, so do not you force men to a religion against their consciences.[36]

Assertions of liberty of conscience in the first decades of the seventeenth century were not confined to well-known leaders of sectarian splinters of the Cambridge Puritan movement. Thomas Palmer, high sheriff of Kent, wrote in 1606 "that no man hath power of religion . . . the liberty whereof resteth in the hands of God only, to dispose of." In his view, conscience could not be compelled, and the prudent state would respect this fact.[37] Henry Jacob, regarded by some as the founder of Congregationalism, spoke often of the liberty of conscience. Like Perkins, he wrote, "We are clearly commanded to obey God rather than man," and what God commanded was known by conscience.[38] Jacob thus pleaded his case for congregational autonomy upon the grounds of conscience. As he did so, he astutely reminded James I of his statements about the consciences of Catholics:

> You have signified that you intend no persecution against them for conscience cause, and that you never laid any thing to the charge of any for cause of conscience. This giveth us to have great hope and confidence, and to comfort ourselves upon the same, your royal word.[39]

Appreciation of the significance of conscience for Protestant Christians grew even faster as the policy of moderate toleration gave way to the repressive attitude of William Laud. John Canne wrote in 1636 that the Established Church was not constituted by or for the saints, rather it was by "profane people, even mockers and contemners of religion." This false church had left no liberty to any man, whether saved or damned; on the contrary, it "compelled and forced all in the name and power of the Antichrist's successors . . . conscience or no conscience."[40]

From the foregoing it is clear that many persons regarded as sectarians actively defended the idea of liberty of conscience, and often they did so in a way that betrayed a debt to the view developed by William Perkins. In addition to these, concern for conscience appeared among a number of persons who remained active members of the English Church, often being themselves clergymen.

From the point of view of the development of the idea of liberty of conscience as stated by William Perkins, the views that will be examined here appear at first to be unrelated. The views of these churchmen, however, contributed to the acceptance of the idea of liberty of conscience in two ways. First, some of them spoke tacitly of conscience as having certain rights, though their view does not seem to be rooted in the works of William Perkins or other Cambridge Puritans. Others did not speak of conscience or its rights, but they did insist that the areas where the church could enforce its views were very limited. In short, the cause of conscience and its liberty under the early Stuarts was aided by the views of some churchmen, views that complemented the claim for liberty of conscience.

A number of important churchmen expressed their belief that the fundamentals of Christianity were limited in number and that only these should be the concern of the church as it sought to keep itself pure. The obvious conclusion is that men were at liberty to believe as they saw fit on other issues. In 1615, for example, Bishop Jegon of Norwich wrote to his superior and asked for permission to prosecute a parishioner, William Sayer, for heresy. After examining the evidence Bishop Abbot wrote back that Sayer had only confused a medley of Separatist, Baptist, and Barrowist doctrines. Significantly he added, "It will never be assented to, that he should burn as a heretic, unless he deny something expressly contained in the three creeds or in the four first general councils."[41]

In the same vein another churchman wrote, "The only fundamental truth in religion is this: that Jesus Christ the son of God, who took our nature from the virgin Mary, is our only and all sufficient savior."[42] Richard Bernard, the author, said further that all who accept this are in the way of salvation. All other teachings of the church are of secondary importance, he added, and tend only to illustrate the one basic truth.

John Donne, more famous as poet than priest, came to the same conclusion. The churches are "virtual beams of one sun," he wrote. No one church had a monopoly; thus, "nothing hinders our own salvation more, than to deny salvation, to all but ourselves." Donne's disposition toward toleration was linked to his belief that men come by their religion more by birth, education, and accident than by intellectual discernment. Religious truth was difficult to obtain, a point he made in one of his poems:

> On a huge hill,/Cragged and steep, Truth stands, and he that will/reach her, about must, and about must go;/And what the hills suddennes resists, win so;/Yet strive so, that before age, deaths twilight,/Thy soul rest, for none can work in that night.[43]

Bishop Joseph Hall treated the problem more fully and made a further distinction between attitudes toward the fundamentals. Only those who err in the plain language of the Apostles' Creed may be considered heretical, a narrower criterion than Bishop Abbot. Heresy considered dangerous by him consisted of two types, that which was passively and privately held, and that which was actively held and propagated. The former was a spiritual sin and had to be dealt with by purely spiritual means. The activist who propagated his views had to be persuaded of his error; that failing, Hall believed that the activist would run afoul of the state and in due course be punished for civil disturbances. For Hall the spirit of man was subject only to God. "Princes and churches may make laws for the outward man, but they can no more bind the heart than they can make it," wrote Hall, in a passage reminiscent of William Perkins.[44]

Thomas Fuller, the seventeenth-century church historian, wrote that the Christian does not believe "in forcing others to his own opinion," but leaves every man to his own liberty.[45] John Randall argued that "Christ would not be defended by the sword; spiritual power betakes itself to better weapons, to spiritual and heavenly weapons." For him, law and force could not impinge upon faith and conscience.[46] Writing in 1630, John Bury spoke his mind on the question of physical force in spiritual affairs when he asked, "Did you ever know any souls converted, any man cured, with such gall and vinegar?"[47] In the same spirit Thomas Adams stated that "there is nothing so voluntary as religion; faith comes by persuasion, not by compulsion." He continued, "Fire and fagot are powerless to give him faith."[48]

Consistent with these arguments was Bishop Downame's observation that "the conscience of a Christian is exempted from human power, and cannot be bound but where God doth bind it."[49] Downame's observation echoes the view of William Perkins, but it is also consistent with the views of his fellow churchmen. For example, he assumes, as do they, that the fundamentals of faith are few, and like them, he assumes that man is bound to observe them.

The question arises as to how to relate the views of the churchmen to the general themes of toleration and liberty of conscience. Within the group of churchmen discussed it would be possible to distinguish a variety of views. Downame's position, for example, appears to be no different from some of the sectarians noted earlier. On the other hand, Bishop Abbot, in judging the case sent to him from Norwich, assumed that denial of certain creeds was grounds for prosecution.

The factor that distinguishes the views of men like Downame from that of Perkins is the question of sphere sovereignty. Failure to posit the authority of conscience in terms that showed a commitment to authority as transcending institutions is the difference between the view of a Downame and Perkins. The view of a Bishop Abbot is clearly a position of toleration, his view being the same as that expressed often among Elizabethan governmental and church officials.

The views of the churchmen, from Bishop Abbot to Bishop Downame, are all expressions of toleration, but they represent an important position in the development of toleration under the early Stuarts. Their views are not consistent with the tone and flavor of a William Laud, especially those such as Joseph Hall and Downame who were active during the years when Laud came to power. It may be conjectured that these men represent a view of toleration that was more consistent with that devised under Elizabeth and followed, more or less, by James I.

In a broad perspective, toleration and liberty of conscience during the period 1600-1640 were in sharper conflict than they had been during the Age of Elizabeth. Toleration as a policy became more harsh and narrow, especially as it was influenced by Bishop Laud. At the same time interest in and concern for liberty of conscience expanded, particularly among splinters of the Cambridge Puritan movement. Their attraction to liberty of conscience was no doubt due to the fact that liberty of conscience inherently assumed the sovereignty of the individual. Liberty of conscience thus could be a powerful tool in the move toward separatism. Finally, a number of men in the English Church advocated views that aided the cause of conscience and its liberty, but these views were not ultimately rooted in the conception of authority and sovereignty that had been stated by William Perkins.

The development of the conflict between the ideas of toleration and liberty was complicated during the period 1600-1640 by the theological creations of a one-time Cambridge Puritan, William Ames. His views deserve special consideration because of their influence on the problem of toleration and liberty of conscience in America.

C. William Ames and the Problem of Conscience

The collective thought of the builders of the Bay Colony has been described as the "New England Mind" by Perry Miller. Important for Miller's scheme were its roots in the thinking of a handful of dissenters who were either driven out of England or chose to leave during the first decades of the seventeenth century. Miller characterized the typical thinking of these Puritans as "orthodoxy," and found that William Ames was the chief architect. Says Miller, "The standard textbook survey of theology used by New England students was William Ames's *Medulla*. . . ."[50]

While Miller made a good case for the connection between Ames's theology and that of early New Englanders, he did not concern himself with the role of conscience in the thought of either Ames or the Bay leaders.[51] An examination of Ames's writings suggests that conscience was not only important in his thinking, but vital to his whole scheme of theology. His view was, moreover, very different from that of Perkins, and thus deserves special attention.

Ames, born in 1576, brought up in a Puritan environment, came to Cambridge late in the 1590's, during Perkins' tenure there.[52] Undoubtedly Ames learned to appreciate the value of and need for practical divinity from the master himself. Ames, like Perkins, wrote a treatise on conscience, complete with a collection of cases of conscience.[53] The similarity between what Perkins and Ames had to say about conscience all but ended with the word *conscience*. The difference between Perkins and Ames has been explained in terms of background and temperament, but the evidence on these points is thin.[54]

While at Cambridge, though after the death of Perkins (1602), Ames demonstrated his tendency toward active non-conformity, a stance not evident in Perkins.[55] For example, at the time of his ordination he refused to wear the usual garb. This performance, coupled with others of the same type, undoubtedly led to his suspension and expulsion "without degrees taken or in process." This non-conformity, too, probably was the factor that caused him to be passed over as new lectureships in Cambridge were assigned.

Ames's Cambridge days were over by 1609, and thereafter he began a new phase of his career. Soon he moved, some say fled, to Holland. As in the case of his stay in Cambridge, little is known of his first ten years in Holland. In that period, however, he did write introductions to new editions of several non-conformist tracts, endorsing the contents.[56] He also served as chief advisor to the moderator in the Synod of Dordt, a tribute to his skill and knowledge in theology. Soon after Dordt, in 1620, Ames became rector of the University of Franeker.[57]

Accession to the rectorship of Franeker began yet another phase of Ames's career, one, however, that displays more clearly his thinking and personal involvement in Puritan reform. Ames's relationship to and influence on the band of men who became leading figures in the founding of Massachusetts Bay Colony occurred during this period, a point that has been adequately documented by Perry Miller.[58]

While at Franeker Ames wrote his two most important books, and they indicate why it was that Ames's view of conscience differed from that of Perkins. During the years 1620-22, Ames lectured to the sons of wealthy Leyden merchants, publishing the substance of these lectures as *Medulla theologica* in 1623; thereafter they appeared in English as *The Marrow of Sacred Divinity*. Ames stated in the "forewarning" that he intended this work, together with a companion volume, later published as *Conscience,* to be a statement of all that was important in theology.[59] He intended, he said, that these works would be of use to all, laymen as well as theological students. To that end he set out the material in a systematic way, with chapter headings and subheadings. This technique would make it easy for one not familiar with theology to find the topic that concerned him most.[60]

Ames's use of headings, subheadings, and sub-subheadings is a clue to the difference between his work and that of Perkins, for these characteristics reflect the application of a new method in theology. This new stance was already evident in Ames's "forewarning," where he stated, "I see several points which will be brought against my well intentioned endeavor."[61] Ames anticipated objections to this system as not being precise enough: "There will be those who will desire a more exact use of the art of logic."[62] Logic! That was the root of his new method in theology.

This new method, that forced Ames to reject Perkins' view of conscience, that forced him to defend himself in the introduction to the *Marrow*, was an adaptation of the new logic of Peter Ramus. It was the process of accommodation and adaptation of the Ramist method to the problems of Puritan thought and theology that produced in Ames's *Marrow* and *Conscience* a distinctive position. Since there are two factors involved here, Ramus' method and Ames's use of it, they will be discussed separately.

Who Ramus was and what influence he had are questions that began to be answered for moderns only in the last decades. Perry Miller tells us that in his execursions into the European background to American Puritanism he was struck by the enoromous literary reference to Peter Ramus.[63] He pieced together a fragmented sketch of what he saw as the influence of Ramus, including it as an appendix to one of his volumes on the New England Mind.[64] There he invited interested scholars to pursue the subject further. A Jesuit, Walter Ong, took up this suggestion and published the results of his studies in 1958.[65] What is known of Ramus at this time depends almost entirely on the work of these two men.

Ramus was born in the province of Picardy in France, six miles from the birthplace of Calvin and six years later than Calvin, in 1515.[66] At the age of twenty-one he startled the learned world by maintaining in his Master of Arts thesis at Paris, "Whatever has been said from Aristotle is forged."[67] From that day until St. Bartholomew's Day in 1572 Ramus wrought a continuous battle against the accepted standards of intellectual activity, fomenting something akin to an intellectual revolution.[68] All through this period he constantly was in danger physically, receiving protection now from some patron and again from some other person of power. Ramus created such a stir that a royal decree banned his writings, and on occasion they were publicly burned. His death was violent, some accounts stating that he was thrown from an upper-story window, while others claiming he was beheaded and cast into the river.[69] "In the eyes of contemporaries," states Perry Miller, "he died equally for the cause of logic and of Christ."[70]

What this Ramist doctrine was that so stirred the minds of men can only be appreciated by reading a full description as found in either Miller or Ong, but the main thrust of his thinking may be stated in a summary fashion.[71] His purpose was to set forth certain key ideas that would enable men to think easily and correctly. Traditionally there were three parts to philosophy—ethics, physics, and dialectic—the latter, according to Ramus, was the only one that need be relied on to assure right thinking. Dialectic could be practiced only after advancing through the levels of grammar and rhetoric, grammar being the first level of communication. Rhetoric was more complex than grammar and was that level of communication in which men attempted to capture the variety of language, its subtleties, poetic expression, nuances, and figures of speech. Dialectic stood at the top level, giving a sense of order to rhetoric. Distracting ideas and irrelevant ones were easily discarded as man reasoned his way to the solution of a problem if dialectic was properly used. Ramus' dialectic was eminently practical, so it was thought, because it drew its problems from real-life situations.

Professor Ong tells us that Ramus was influenced by Rudolph Agricola (1443-1485) in departing from Aristotle, and that from Agricola Ramus learned that dialectic consisted of invention and judgment.[72] It was in the use of the concept of invention that the unique features of Ramism had its roots. Ong gives the example of man wanting to know if he is dialectical.[73] To obtain an affirmative answer, or a negative one, Aristotelian categories[74] need not be applied. Here was one of the enchanting features of the new method, for in Aristotelian terms the use of categories necessitated knowledge of some other field, one that might be totally unfamiliar. How did one reach the answer without using the old system? The question was composed of two parts—man, the minor, and dialectical, the major. In some way they could be joined if the answer was affirmative. Contrariwise, if they could not be joined, the answer was negative. In the case at hand, a connection might be made by "inventing" or finding a term that linked man and dialectic. In

Ramism this link was called an "argument" or middle term.[75] Significantly this argument was descriptive in the sense of reflecting, rather than the usual sense of the word *argument* as it is used in *controversy*. Logic in this scheme becomes a search for the proper link between the major and minor elements in a given question. The question posed by Ong in the example was resolved by suggesting that the argument or middle term is "rational."[76] The factor would be stated in a simple syllogism; thus, "Whatever is rational is dialectical; every man is rational; therefore, man is dialectical."[77] The simple question in this manner has an affirmative answer.

The crucial feature in this system is the matter of finding or inventing the middle term. Early, Ramus solved this problem by composing a list of "arguments" that might be employed; in time he expanded its length.[78] Of course, on occasion, it might be necessary to reach a final conclusion by breaking the original question up into a series of questions. On the other hand, with some questions the argument came immediately to mind without recourse to a list of topics or arguments. Skill in the use of this method forced students of Ramus to create ever larger lists of topics and the result was, as Ong points out, the formation of the modern encyclopedia.[79]

Judgment was the second part of Ramus' dialectic, and is basically an expansion of the process of invention. It involved the art of separating the major and minor parts of the question. This could be accomplished by induction, a skillful use of topic, or the employment of religious teachings. The use of judgment in this sense resulted in those divisions and subdivisions, and sub-subdivisions that mark every Ramistically influenced work.[80]

Looking again into Ames's works, one is made aware of the fact that they bear a character and form markedly Ramist. Ames's practice of dividing his subject into parts, a practice noted several times already, is nothing else than the application of Ramus' method. The result, of course, was that theology—the study of how to live for God—divided into "faith" and observance," each in turn being sub- and sub-subdivided until all[81] possible topics relating to theology had been included in the scheme.

The subject of conscience[82] is another example of how Ames applied Ramist method to theology, but as will be evident, his use of it here had far reaching results for the meaning of conscience. He defined conscience simply as "man's judgment of himself according to the judgment of God of him."[83] From the point of view of Ramist influence, however, much more is involved. First, such a brief definition itself is characteristically Ramist. Any good Ramist could show his reader how he reached a clear and concise statement, but the contents of statements were most important. Ames's definition of conscience in this way is the same kind of definition found in the Ong example, "man is dialectical."[84] Such statements could become exceedingly sterile as educational devices, and they did in time, but to the practicing Ramist such statements conjured up the whole process that led to the statement.

In the opening pages of *Conscience* Ames reviews the history of definitions of conscience,[85] and raises the question whether conscience belongs to apprehension or to discourse. His answer:

> It belongs to judgment discoursing, because it cannot do its act of accusing, excusing, comforting unless it be through the means of some third argument, whose force appeareth only in a Syllogism, by that which is deduced and concluded out of it.[86]

Recalling that *Conscience* was a companion to the earlier work *Marrow*, it could be concluded that Ames was referring to the same form of argument he used in the earlier work. That this was his intention emerges even more clearly in the example he gives in the passage immediately following the statement just quoted. He says:

> The force and nature of conscience therefore is contained in such a syllogism. He that lives in sin, shall die;/ I live in sin;/ Therefore, I shall die.[87]

Here he is saying that conscience by nature expresses itself in the syllogism; he is more precise a few lines down when he states that in the "syllogism alone is contained the whole nature of conscience."[88] In short, conscience was dialectic.

Professor Eusden in his thoughtful introduction to a new translation of Ames's *Marrow* has captured the significance of Ames's use of conscience as dialectic, his observations including useful examples.⁸⁹ Eusden correctly points out that employment of the dialectic method to the field of morals through conscience posed the possibility of Ames bringing order to the field of moral problems.⁹⁰ Ames's *Conscience* is written with a tone and flavor that suggests he was confident that he would bring a sense of order to moral problems. Eusden came to the same conclusion, as is evident in several of his comments. The book *Conscience*, says Eusden, "is really an attempt to apply the Ramus dialectic to what Ames considers the key problems of social and personal life." Further, "Ames seldom, however, uses the word *dialectic;* he prefers his own word 'conscience' which he views as the dialectical method in action."⁹¹ According to Eusden the "invention" and "judgment" of the dialectic process became operative in conscience, these describing that ability of moral man to make decisions.⁹² This process can be readily seen in Ames's discussion of conscience and its problems, though the special place that Scripture occupied required some adjustments in the scheme of pure dialectic.

The process of "invention" and "judgment" in conscience, for Ames, was different than it had been in pure dialectic, a change that was tied to the special place the Bible occupied in matters moral. Natural man had a conscience whose dictates were binding; the Bible, however, placed additional demands upon the conscience.⁹³ In demonstrating how this worked, Ames derived two types of biblical injunctions, both of which he refers to as "law" or "light."⁹⁴ In the syllogism these correspond to the major proposition. A "law" derived from a passage of the Decalogue is just as important for Ames as one drawn from a whole block of passages. "No murder" is thus a binding "law" as "covenant" obligations are binding, the former, a specific point in Exodus 20, the latter, the "obvious" rule given in the whole long story of Abraham.⁹⁵

Ames is not particularly concerned about the problems of conscience that natural man experiences. Presumably its operation serves to convict him of his sin, leaving him in a state of anguish until he comes to know what the Bible can do to bring him peace. Natural man's conscience will derive a law from nature that will tell him that murder, for example, is evil.⁹⁶

Most of Ames's discussion of conscience demonstrates how one works from the "law," whether specific or general, to personal application. Typical is the example he gives in the first pages of *Conscience*.[97] One may ask, "Do I have eternal life?" The "light" of Scripture is, "Whoever believes in Christ shall not die, but live." The "witness" is, "I believe in Christ." The conclusion follows, "Therefore, I shall not die, but live."[98] As in his general theology, Ames uses the Ramist method to arrive at a quick and certain answer.

Ames's identification of conscience as dialectic had profound implications for the liberty of conscience. It may be argued that his identification of conscience as dialectic precluded—if it had not foreclosed—the possibility of or need for liberty of conscience. Recall again Ramus and his method. Ramus' intent was to establish a more sure guide to intellectual activity, and he found the answer in dialectic. This was a system that by its character could potentially arrange all possible problems of thought into a unitary universe of discourse. With the stress on system and unity in Ramus' dialectic, identification of conscience as dialectic by Ames locked conscience to a method that by its nature projected an aura of determinism into the field of moral problems. Stated another way, reliance upon conscience when it was a comprehensive method eliminated the need to think in terms of conscience as something that could have liberty.

The sense of determinism evident in Ames's view of conscience appeared also in the title of his book *Conscience*. He used the word *law* in the subtitle in the sense of predictable results.[99] It is difficult to avoid the conclusion that in Ames's view all moral problems had predictable answers, that there was a law or rule to cover each and every case of conscience. All that was necessary was the use of the dialectic syllogism, that is, conscience. In such a view it is not necessary to speak of liberty of conscience; indeed, to do so would appear to be beyond comprehension.

Ames's application of the Ramist method to the definition of conscience placed him outside of the tradition of William Perkins, and the question must be asked as to how he relates to the general development of the conflict between the idea of toleration and liberty of conscience. From the foregoing it is clear that he did not advocate liberty of conscience, but a moment's reflection reveals the fact that he taught a system that placed conscience on the same ground as that occupied by the idea of toleration. In locking conscience to method, method became authoritative in the same way that the government was in its policy of toleration. In terms of sphere sovereignty Ames's position is more difficult to characterize, but it is clear that he advocated a view that stripped the individual of his liberty.

The implication of Ames's system in practice became evident in the Massachusetts Bay Colony as it faced the problem of dissent. The treatment of dissenters and the proximity of the spheres of the state and the church betray a commitment to a system that was fundamentally no different from the prevailing system in England.

D. *Conclusion*

During the period 1600-1640 three important developments occurred that were to have profound influence upon the conflict between the ideas of toleration and liberty of conscience in the years ahead. First, toleration under the early Stuarts continued as a policy, but during the reign of Charles it became more narrow and repressive, especially as it was influenced by William Laud. Second, the claim of liberty of conscience was actively advocated by an increasing number of people, particularly among the leaders of the sectarian splinters of the Cambridge Puritan movement. The cause of conscience was also aided by some churchmen through their insistence on the validity of viewing the fundamentals of religion as limited in number. Some of these men even spoke of conscience as having certain rights, but their view differed from that of Perkins in that they did not base their conception of conscience upon the idea of sphere sovereignty. Third, the writings of William Ames during the period spawned a new view of conscience, one that was to have profound implications for the development of the conflict between toleration and liberty of conscience in America. Ames wrote a long treatise about conscience and its problems, but it did not advocate liberty of conscience. It could not foster this idea because his notion of conscience was tied to the Ramist method of dialectic, the method becoming authoritative for the treatment of the affairs of conscience. Ames's view was thus, in fact, no different from the advocates of toleration, for the individual in his system was stripped of his liberty in matters of conscience. In short, the divisions among Englishmen concerning conscience that emerged during the Age of Elizabeth became more pronounced during the period 1600-1640. The developments during this period affected many of the major political and religious disputes in the two decades following 1640. The attitude of Ames toward conscience, on the other hand, affected the political and religious affairs of the Massachusetts Bay Colony. The place of the Amesian attitude toward conscience in that colony is a central theme in the next chapter.

CHAPTER NOTES

1. C. H. McIlwain, ed., *The Political Works of James I* (Cambridge, Mass., 1918), pp. 7-8.
2. *Ibid.*
3. *Ibid.*
4. Jordan, *Toleration*, II, p. 32.
5. McIlwain, *James I*, p. 322.
6. Jordan, *Toleration*, II, p. 54.
7. *Ibid.*, p. 90 ff.
8. *Ibid.*, p. 169 ff.
9. *Ibid.*
10. *Ibid.*
11. *Ibid.*, p. 132.
12. Maurice Ashley, *Great Britain to 1688* (Ann Arbor, 1961), pp. 331-332.
13. *Ibid.*, p. 332.
14. *Ibid.*
15. Jordan, *Toleration*, II, p. 117 ff.
16. *Ibid.*
17. *Ibid.*
18. *Ibid.*
19. John Rushworth, *Historical Collections* (London, 1659-1701), I, pp. 604-605.
20. *Ibid.*, p. 645.
21. *Ibid.*
22. Jordan, *Toleration*, II, p. 162.
23. *Ibid.*, pp. 138-142.
24. Edmund S. Morgan, *Visible Saints: The History of a Puritan Idea* (Ithaca, 1963), is a standard interpretation.
25. John Smyth, *Confession of Faith* (London, 1611), Art. lxxxvi.
26. John Robinson, *Works* (London, 1851), I, p. 41.
27. *Ibid.*
28. Thomas Helwys, *A Declaration of Faith* (London, 1611), Art. xxiv.
29. Thomas Helwys, *An Advertisement, or Admonition Unto the Congregation* (London, 1611), p. 58.
30. Thomas Helwys, *A Short Declaration of the Mystery of Iniquity* (London, 1612), p. 37.
31. *Ibid.*
32. *Ibid.*, p. 41.
33. *Ibid.*
34. E. B. Underhill, ed., *Tracts on Liberty of Conscience and Persecution* (London, 1846), p. 1 ff.

35. *Ibid.*
36. Leonard Busher, *Religious Peace: or, A Plea for Liberty of Conscience* (London, 1614), p. 68.
37. Thomas Palmer, *An Essay of the Means How to Make Our Travels* (London, 1606), p. 110.
38. Henry Jacob, *A Confession and Protestation* (Amsterdam, 1612), Art. xxviii.
39. *Ibid.*, but before text of Confession, p. 47.
40. John Canne, *A Light for the Ignorant* (London, 1636), pp. 9, 15.
41. Jordan, *Toleration*, II, p. 35.
42. Richard Bernard, *Christian Advertisements and Councils of Peace* (London, 1608), p. 174.
43. Quoted in Jordan, *Toleration*, II, p. 40.
44. Joseph Hall, *Works* (London, 1863), VI, p. 649.
45. Thomas Fuller, *The Holy and Profane State* (London, 1831), p. 66.
46. John Randall, *Twenty-nine Lectures on the Church* (London, 1636), II, p. 91.
47. John Bury, *The Moderate Christian* (London, 1631), p. 11.
48. Thomas Adams, *Works* (London, 1629), p. 559.
49. George Downame, *The Christians Freedom* (London, 1635), pp. 102, 104 ff.
50. *N.E.M.*, I, p. 48.
51. For an excellent discussion of other themes ignored by Miller see George M. Marsden's "Perry Miller's Rehabilitation of the Puritans: A Critique," *Church History*, XXXIX (March, 1970), p. 92.
52. Hugo Visscher, *William Ames: His Life and Works*, Douglas Horton, tr. (Cambridge, Mass., 1956), p. 29. This brief item is bound with two others translated by Horton. It is distributed by the Harvard Divinity School Library.
53. *Ibid.*, and J. D. Eusden's edition of Ames's *Marrow of Theology* (Boston, 1968), pp. 1-3, lists some of the editions of Ames's writings on conscience.
54. Hugo Visscher, *William Ames: His Life and Works*, pp. 29-31, argues for a difference in background and temperament.
55. *Ibid.*
56. Perry Miller, *Orthodoxy in Massachusetts 1630-1650* (Cambridge, 1933), p. 79.
57. William Ames, *Marrow of Theology*, J. D. Eusden, tr. (Boston, 1968), is the edition that has been used, hereinafter cited as Ames, *Marrow*. See p. 3 ff. for a review of Ames's career.
58. Miller, *Orthodoxy*, chap. V.
59. Ames, *Marrow*, p. 67. Ames's book, *Conscience: Its Law or Cases, Five Books* (London, 1643), is a rare item. I have used one that belongs to the Westminster Theological Seminary, Philadelphia, Pa.

60. Ames, *Marrow*, p. 67 ff.
61. *Ibid.*, p. 69.
62. *Ibid.*
63. Miller, *N.E.M.*, I, chap. V and Appendix A.
64. *Ibid.*
65. Walter Ong, *Ramus Method and the Decay of Dialogue* (Cambridge, Mass., 1958).
66. The sketch of Ramus here is a consolidation of facts mentioned by either Ong, Miller, or Eusden. His proximity to Calvin's birthplace was not mentioned by any of them, however.
67. *N.E.M.*, I, p. 116.   69. *Ibid.*
68. *Ibid.*   70. *Ibid.*
71. Eusden's summary of Ramus is particularly pithy.
72. Ong, *Ramus Method*. See and compare pp. 42-45, 92-96, and 182-190.
73. *Ibid.*, pp. 182-190.
74. Discussion of the problem of categories in thought-systems is a complex matter. An entree to the problem may be made by examining Dagobert D. Runes's *Dictionary of Philosophy* (Ames, Iowa, 1955), p. 47; W. Windelband, *History of Ancient Philosophy* (New York, 1957), p. 256 ff.; Richard McKeon, *The Basic Works of Aristotle* (New York, 1941), pp. xvi-xvii, pp. 7-37; and Werner Jaeger, *Aristotle* (Oxford, 1955). For the best and most readable discussion of this problem see Herman Dooyeweerd, *A New Critique of Theoretical Thought* (Philadelphia, 1958), II, for specific reference to Aristotle, see p. 445 ff.
75. Ong, *Ramus Method*, p. 182.
76. *Ibid.*   78. *Ibid.*, p. 183.   80. *Ibid.*, p. 202.
77. *Ibid.*   79. *Ibid.*   81. Ames, *Marrow*, p. 77.
82. One could construct a chart of the sub-division of conscience, the point being that it was treated by Ames as one more part or subject of theology.
83. Ames, *Conscience*, bk. 1, p. 1.
84. Compare Ames's *Conscience*, bk. 1, p. 1, with Ong, *Ramus Method*, pp. 182-183.
85. Ames, *Conscience*, bk. 1, pp. 1-8.
86. *Ibid.*, p. 3.   91. *Ibid.*, p. 42.
87. *Ibid.*   92. *Ibid.*
88. *Ibid.*, p. 4.   93. Ames, *Conscience*, bk. 1, pp. 5-6.
89. Ames, *Marrow*, p. 42 ff.   94. *Ibid.*
90. *Ibid.*
95. Professor Eusden discusses this problem lucidly. See Ames, *Marrow*, p. 44.
96. Ames, *Conscience*, bk. 1, p. 5.   97. *Ibid.*, p. 3.
98. Ames, *Marrow*, pp. 44-45.
99. See J. D. Eusden's comment in Ames, *Marrow*, p. 8, n. 15.

Chapter III

CONSCIENCE AND THE BUILDERS OF THE BAY COLONY: 1630-1640

The first colonists came to New England to enjoy liberty of conscience, or so many have believed. As early as 1730 an essayist in *American Weekly Mercury* could ask, "Is it not shocking that the same people who left their native country to enjoy liberty of conscience should turn persecutors as soon as they were in power?" This question by the Reverend Josiah Smith was answered in the next breath affirmatively, "Yet this is true of many who went to New England . . . to avoid persecution."[1] Smith's view, that the founders of New England came to enjoy liberty of conscience, was not an isolated case, for in the next year the Governor of Massachusetts spoke to the General Court these words, "One great errand of our fathers hither was to avoid all impositions on their conscience. . . ."[2] This view that the enjoyment of liberty of conscience was a prime factor in the founding of New England has persisted to the present time.[3]

As a matter of fact, the prime motive for the founding of New England, particularly Massachusetts, was exactly the opposite of that stated by the Reverend Smith and Governor Belcher. Stated positively, the purpose of the Bay Colony was to create a society in which there would be no need or room for liberty of conscience.

Governor Winthrop, in his famous lay-sermon on the *Arbella*, while the main body of leaders of the new Bay Colony were in transit, stated clearly enough what their purpose was. The most-quoted lines of this famous speech comment on their purpose:

> . . . To seek out a place of cohabitation and consortship under a due form of government both civil and ecclesiastical. . . . For we must consider that we shall be as a city upon a hill, the eyes of all people are upon us; so if we shall deal falsely . . . we shall

be made a story and a by-word of many of God's worthy servants. . . .[4]

It is obvious that Winthrop was conscious of being involved in the establishment of a new society. Noteworthy, however, is the fact that these lines do not state that the new society was intended as a haven for the religiously persecuted, that men would be at liberty in the new form of government "both civil and ecclesiastical" to do as they pleased. Other lines in Winthrop's speech indicate that the purpose was more nearly the opposite. Speaking of their experiment he said, "In such cases as this the care of the public must oversway all private aspects."[5]

Winthrop's assertion that the new colony was a city upon a hill and that public interests must over-ride private ones pointed toward the need for uniformity among the people of the Bay Colony. If they were to succeed as an example of what a Christian society should be, it was especially important that there be unanimity among the leaders, and it was vital, too, that there be unanimity among the general citizenry.[6] In this context deviations from an agreed or assumed orthodoxy were a critical problem for the young colony.

While there have been some objections to minor themes in the writings of Perry Miller on New England Puritanism, the essential character of the New England mind he has outlined may be regarded as correct, including the influence of William Ames on this pattern of thought. Noted earlier was the relationship between Ames and the circle of people that gathered around him in Holland, many of them migrating subsequently to New England. This association, coupled with the observations of Miller as to the influence of Amesian ideas on early New England, documents a close tie between Ames and the character of what Miller has called "orthodoxy" in Massachusetts.

In addition to a general acceptance of Amesian theology in the Massachusetts Bay Colony, the colony accepted and practiced Ames's view of conscience. Two episodes in the first decade of this colony's experience demonstrate the Amesian view of conscience in practice. The dispute with and treatment of Roger Williams is a clear illustration of the application of Ames's view. The Antinomian controversy, particularly as it affected Anne Hutchinson, is a second example of the disposition of Massachusets Bay leaders to rely on the Amesian view of conscience as they attempted to maintain uniformity.

Before turning to a discussion of the practice of Amesian principles of conscience in Massachusetts Bay Colony, it will be useful to review certain peculiarities evident in Ames's position on the problem of conscience. The single most important feature of the Amesian view of conscience was the fact that it was tied to the dialectic method, the method acting in an authoritative capacity as problems of conscience were solved. Use of this method eliminated the need to think in terms of conscience as having liberty. From another perspective, Ames taught that conscience was not so much an internal function of the self as it was an external process regulated by a rational dialectic method. While Ames himself did not speak of *liberty* of conscience, such a concept being unnecessary in a system where all problems of conscience could be outlined and solved through the application of method, the use of this phrase appeared among his followers in Massacusetts Bay. The use of the concept was so different, however, that it in fact had no relationship to the concept as stated by William Perkins and others. As will be evident, liberty of conscience in the Amesian system was liberty to believe orthodoxy. This distinction is important because it would be easy to confuse the views of Ames and Perkins among Massachusetts Bay leaders on the question of conscience. The nub of the difference turns on the meaning of the phrase "liberty of conscience."

The problem of conscience among Massachusetts Bay leaders, that is, the question of whether they followed Ames or Perkins, has also been colored by the fact that Ames has been traditionally associated with the group of sectarians discussed earlier. While Ames was an outcast from the established church, and thus, in a sense at least, sectarian, his distinctive theological creations set him apart from other sectarians, especially in the matter of conscience. Ames's view of conscience was much closer to that of traditional churchmen than it was to that of a Henry Jacob.[7]

To emphasize, Ames, and thus "orthodoxy in Massachusetts," did not embrace liberty of conscience as conceived of by William

Perkins. In matters of conscience the only alternative was some system of toleration, and Massachusetts Bay leaders hammered out a policy of toleration as their orthodoxy was challenged during the years following 1630. In this they were no different from the government of England, a point illustrated by Winthrop when he said "the care of the public must over-sway all private respects."

A. *Roger Williams*

Majestic marble monuments of the heroes of the Calvinistic Reformation stand in Geneva, Switzerland. Central in the arrangement are the greatest heroes—Calvin, Farel, Beza, and Knox. On either side stand warriors who fought in other nations—Gustavus Adolphus of Sweden, Holland's William the Silent, Coligny of France, and Cromwell of England. Space provided for an American representative is not filled, as one might expect, by John Winthrop, John Cotton, or even Jonathan Edwards, or a latter-day figure such as Charles Hodge, or B. B. Warfield. Such expectations, however great, suffer disappointment, and even bafflement, for in the place provided for the leading figure of American Calvinism stands none other than Roger Williams.[8]

Whether Roger Williams should be enshrined as the representative of American Calvinism may be debated. Perry Miller in a colorful passage has suggested that Winthrop and Cotton have been "heaving in their graves ever since that monument was erected."[9] Williams deserves to be associated with the cause of liberty, however, whatever his relationship to Calvinism may have been. His disputes with his brethren in New England indicate his thinking and contribution to the cause of liberty of conscience.

Early in this century it was a widely circulated idea that Williams was the first American democrat, and an "irrepressible" one at that.[10] American liberals, such as Vernon L. Parrington, focused and fostered this picture of Williams, and their argument seemed to carry import when they contrasted him with what they called the reactionary defenders of Old World politics, such as Winthrop and Cotton. That such a reading of Williams was the result of wishful thinking, if not a severe twisting of the facts, has been more than adequately demonstrated by more serious students of the Puritan mind.[11] Williams' purported political views must be mentioned if only to dismiss them, for it is only when one realizes that Williams was not concerned about political democracy that his true motivation can be understood.

Williams was a religious man, a deeply religious man, and some sense of this inner drive may be grasped by analyzing two characteristics evident in his relationship to Massachusetts Bay leaders and their experiment. Williams had much to say about particular practices as they were instituted and carried on in the colonies, his view of them being one characteristic feature of his differences with Bay leadership. A second feature of Williams' relationship involved the form of argument that he used in the disputes, though it was not consciously identified as a difference by either party.

The Massachusetts Bay Colony was a serious religious experiment, and its early leaders appreciated serious and earnest young preachers like Roger Williams. Soon after his arrival in 1631 Williams was invited by the Boston Church to officiate in the absence of John Wilson, who had returned to England. Williams was invited because his arrival was preceded by reports of his ability as a preacher and Bible scholar, no small honor for one twenty-seven years old.[12]

To the surprise of the Boston Church, Williams refused to accept the offer. His reason for declining shows that at an early date Williams was determined to pursue the goal of a pure church as he understood it. He declined the offer because the Boston Church had not renounced its communion with the Church of England, something he had done.[13]

Refusal to officiate in the Boston Church was only the first of several practical steps taken by Williams as he proceeded down the road that would lead ultimately to banishment from the Bay colony. Williams left Boston and subsequently accepted an invitation from the Salem Church to be its teacher. Winthrop states in his *Journal* that the General Court was concerned that Salem could accept Williams in light of his refusal to preach for the Boston Church. In the same passage Winthrop records additional observations which show that Bay leaders began to sense that this earnest young preacher posed something of a threat to Bay orthodoxy. The Court wrote to John

Endicott, the leading figure in Salem, and, according to Winthrop, informed him that the new teacher had ". . . declared his opinion that the magistrate might not punish the breach of the Sabbath, nor any other offense, as it was a breach of the first table [of the ten commandments]."[14]

Soon Williams left Salem, though it is not clear that his departure had anything to do with the Court's letter to Endicott. Williams next appeared in Plymouth, and in time returned again to Salem, where he led private meetings for devotion and instruction.[15]

By the time Williams had returned to Salem, three years had passed since he came to New England, and during that time many new pastors and teachers had arrived, among them John Cotton and Thomas Hooker. Williams' strange behavior over the past three years was an increasing cause for concern among Massachusetts Bay leaders; now, with the help of these new and prestigious divines, an effort would be made to challenge Williams. Before formal court proceedings against Williams were instituted, John Cotton had read a tract of Williams on the question of whether the king had the right to dispense land in the New World. It was Cotton's opinion that the view of Williams in the tract was not as bad or dangerous as had been represented by word of mouth.[16] The particulars of Cotton's view on the land question are not important except to note the fact that Cotton did not see any immediate cause for alarm.

Notwithstanding Cotton, Bay leaders indicted Williams on four counts and brought him to trial. On the charge involving the question of the king's right to dispense land in the New World, Williams claimed that the king did not have this right, that the land belonged to the Indians. A second disputed Williams' claim that non-Christians should not be required to pray or take an oath. Another raised the issue disputed upon Williams' arrival, the question of separation from the Church of England. The final count in the indictment involved Williams' claim that civil magistrates had no power to enforce the first table of the law, the opinion that the Court had informed Endicott about when the Salem Church invited Williams to be its teacher.[17] The Court was willing to give Williams a week to prepare a defense of these points, but he demurred and demanded a debate immediately.

Hooker, Winthrop states, was appointed to debate with Williams; apparently Hooker carried the day, for Williams was sentenced to banishment.[18]

The bill of particulars on which Williams was indicted shows the areas that Williams believed needed change in the Massachusetts Bay Colony's experiment. When Williams' suggestions for change are compared with the actual program of the Colony, it is obvious that from the Bay leaders' point of view he was a radical. Of special interest is the difference on the question of the relationship between church and state. Williams maintained that the church should be separated from civil power, especially concerning those matters that related to the essence of religion, matters that were covered in the first table of the law. Williams' interest in the separation of the spheres of jurisdiction and responsibility that pertained to the church and state echoes the position spelled out by William Perkins. While Williams came to the same conclusion as Perkins about liberty of conscience and sphere sovereignty, his arguments on these issues were intimately involved in his distinctive hermeneutics.

Hermeneutics being the science of interpretation of the Scriptures, there was a difference between the hermeneutics of Massachusetts Bay leaders and that of Williams. Perry Miller, in his editorial essay appended to the collected writings of Roger Williams, draws a sharp distinction between Williams' hermeneutic principles and those of the Bay's leadership. Miller suggests that Reformation thinkers believed they had moved beyond the simple typological position that had cropped up in the Middle Ages, the leaders of the Bay Colony in Massachusetts following in their footsteps, in Miller's view. From this perspective Miller saw the obvious emphasis in Williams on the typological hermeneutics as a radical departure from the traditional Reformed practice of a John Cotton.[19]

To anyone familiar with Reformed theology Miller's sharp distinction is readily identified as overdrawn. Students of Puritanism have only recently come to appreciate the exaggeration of Miller's distinction. A recent study by Jesper Rosenmeier of the Williams-Cotton controversy takes a step in the right direction toward correcting the sharp difference suggested by Professor Miller.[20] Rosenmeier, citing a study by Sacvan Bercovitch on typology,[21] concludes that all the Divines of New England employed the typological hermeneutics. While this conclusion helps to correct the interpretation of Miller, it does not erase the fact that Williams drew upon the typological method to argue for separation of church and state and for liberty of conscience.

In a society that depended upon the Bible as the source of information and authority for matters of political and social affairs, the special emphasis that Williams placed upon the typological hermeneutics was more than a matter of hair-splitting. The weight that a person assigned to the typological argument could alter profoundly the conclusions that one reached on virtually every major biblical doctrine. The dispute between Williams and John Cotton thus provides a clue to the difference a stronger emphasis upon typology could make regarding biblical doctrines.

For convenience it will help to distinguish between the views of Williams and Massachusetts Bay leaders by employing "federalism" and "typology" to indicate the respective views of the colony's leaders and Williams. Briefly, "federalism" describes the system of theology that came to full bloom in seventeenth-century New England, a system that lays great stress upon the covenant idea. From the perspective of the debate with Roger Williams the covenant idea provided a bridge between the two testaments, allowing theologians to draw upon the Old Testament for examples and patterns to a much greater degree than was customary for writers such as Calvin. The devotion to this view in New England, particularly in the Massachusetts Bay Colony, may be seen in the determination of leaders to attempt to create "a due form of government" that was as close to the example of Mosaic Israel as circumstances would allow. Typological arguments could still be used in the context of federalism, but they were regulated by the over-arching principle of the covenant.

Typology, as emphasized by Williams on the other hand, saw much of the Old Testament as figurative of what was to come in the New Testament. Typology called for greater stress upon the New Testament in the view of Roger Williams. From this perspective the political-religious axis in Israel was supplanted when Christ ushered in a new age, one in which the real power for the believer was spiritual.[22] Williams' greater typological emphasis upon the New Testament was an important factor in his argument with the Massachusetts Bay Colony over the questions of church and state and liberty of conscience.

That liberty of conscience was a central consideration in Williams' mind, and that Bay leaders had a very definite view on this question did not emerge until after Williams had been banished, and he and Cotton entered a "tract-war" on the subject. The extent and scope of these exchanges may be followed in the collected written works of Cotton and Williams,[23] though no systematic study has yet been focused on this problem. Unravelling the pattern of correspondence and publication in an attempt to determine what stage of argument occurred at what point in time is complicated by the fact that Williams often included the latest word by Cotton in the text of a current argument.[24]

It is not difficult, however, to isolate clear statements by each which indicate their respective views. Larzer Ziff has shown how Cotton was introduced to the problem of liberty of conscience in New England.[25] In 1635, at the same time Williams was being tried, Cotton received a letter from England asking his opinion on a treatise that had been enclosed. The subject of the treatise was persecution for cause of conscience. Noting that it was not unusual for a scholar of Cotton's reputation to be queried in such a matter, Ziff observes the irony in the situation:

> How utterly appropriate it was, he was not fully to appreciate until some ten years later, for Roger Williams was eventually to create his masterpiece not only on that topic but as a refutation of Cotton's handling of it.[26]

In his answer to this letter from England on the subject of persecution for cause of conscience, Cotton does not see the main issue as one of liberty of conscience; that issue he discusses only on the last page of his answer.

The substance of Cotton's letter is a patient dividing and subdividing of issues, distinguishing between those that are essential to salvation and those that are not, reminiscent of Ames. Religious practices can be divided in the same manner, according to Cotton. The key to his view, however, may be found in his position on how conscience is informed. At one point he states, "Let me add this one distinction more: When we are persecuted for *Conscience* sake, it is either for conscience rightly informed, or for erroneous and blind conscience."[27] Notwithstanding other points Cotton made in this letter, the central issue was the matter of what he meant by "rightly informed."

Exercising his conception of "rightly informed," Cotton proceeds to maintain that no one should be persecuted for standing on his "rightly informed" conscience, nor, he adds, should anyone be persecuted for an erroneous and blind conscience. Professors of orthodoxy, in this view, could not be lawfully persecuted. Speaking of the erroneous and blind conscience, Cotton said that it needed to be informed rightly, and by that he meant instructed by a wise and orthodox man such as himself. This view allowed Cotton to conclude:

> If such a man after such admonition shall still persist in the error of his way, and be therefore punished, he is not persecuted for cause of conscience, but for sinning against his own conscience.[28]

In a circumstantial matter Cotton was willing to allow the erroneous person lattitude until more light could be shed on the issue, but this was not liberty, for the standard of judgment in that question, as well in the matter of fundamentals, was orthodoxy.

Cotton's only mention of liberty of conscience occurred at the end of his letter, and his comment was an answer to matters that the questioner considered "main objections." Cotton wrote:

> Finally, you come to answer some main objections, as you call them, which are yet by one, and that one objecteth nothing against what we hold. It is (say you) no prejudice to the commonwealth, if liberty of conscience were suffered to such as fear God indeed. . . . But we readily grant you, liberty of conscience is to be granted to men that fear God indeed. . . .[29]

In themselves, these comments by Cotton do not alter the substance of what he had already said, namely, that matters of conscience are bound to the problem of whether it is rightly informed. "Liberty of conscience . . . suffered to such as fear God" was another way of saying saints should not be persecuted, saints being men of orthodoxy.

Cotton's view of conscience stands directly in the tradition of William Ames. The dependence upon the notion of "rightly informed" in Cotton's answer to the problem is nothing more than an application of Ames's argument on the problem of heresy. Ames stipulated in the fourth book of *Conscience* the conditions under which one was determined to be a heretic:

> When the truth is not only manifestly revealed in Scripture, but is also sufficiently propounded . . . unto him, yet doth so adhere to his error, that he either opposeth himself to the plain Scripture, and (sic) [or] will not through the naughtness of his mind perceive the sense of it. . . .[30]

Ames indicates in the same context that he is willing to give the wrongly informed person a chance to be properly informed, this being the same point Cotton makes concerning "erroneous" consciences.

Cotton's letter shows his debt to the view of conscience set forth by Ames. The technique of dividing the question, while not as extreme as in some of Ames's arguments, is the Ramist method. More important is his view that conscience had to be rightly informed, and that the character of the information could be supplied by a system of doctrine or one of its spokesmen. There was no room for the possibility that the individual had to finally decide what he saw as truth in the situation. If conscience was dragged into the process of properly informing a person, and the person resisted the information supplied, the resistance was sin against the individual's conscience. Further, Cotton appears to be uncomfortable with the idea of liberty of conscience. He acknowledges the idea, but does not conceive of it as a right. He calls liberty of conscience a grant, and it is something that may be granted only to those who fear God. In other words, Cotton says that when a man adheres to orthodoxy, he has liberty of conscience.

To emphasize, Cotton's view of conscience as set forth in this letter does not evidence any of the spirit suggested in William

Perkins' statement that Christ has given a liberty to conscience in the New Testament. There is no sense of the spirit of Christian freedom that is the birthright of the re-born Christian. On the contrary, Cotton labors the question of conscience in a tone of one who has to conjure up a rationale for an idea that is foreign to him. Cotton's attitude toward conscience lacked the vigor and vitality evident in Perkins because his view was based upon that of William Ames, because he allowed the problem of conscience to be dominated by the dialectic method. The difference between Cotton's essentially Amesian view of conscience and one that stood in the tradition of Perkins becomes clear when it is compared with the view of Roger Williams.

It was more than a decade after Cotton penned his letter to the English inquirer that Roger Williams published his first statement on the problem of liberty of conscience.[31] Williams wrote profusely and in a style that was less than engaging. His writings, too, were colored by the rapidly changing events of English society. Moreover, his discussion of New England's Way was a twofold argument, the one, examining the cause of his banishment, and the other, investigating persecution and liberty of conscience. At times these two arguments are related, though at most points they are not.[32]

Williams' arguments against persecution and for liberty of conscience were tied to his version of typology. The most advantageous use of this device involved the fourth count of the indictment against Williams at his trial, that is, the question of whether civil magistrates had biblical authority to enforce the first table of the Decalogue. Williams said they did not have this authority, while the Bay leaders claimed that power for magistrates. The crux of this dispute involved a conflict between the answer given in the Old Testament and that given in the New. The Bay leaders, of course, cited the example of Israel. Emphasizing the typological argument, Williams argued that Israel's experience was only a figure and not to be followed. Williams, however, did not rest his case on that point. He challenged Cotton to show him an example in the New Testament that supported their view. Specifically, he asked to be shown the place in which Christ had commanded his followers either to obey magistrates' injunctions concerning religious matters, or to set up a society in which magistrates had authority in religious affairs.[33] Williams did not rest his case on the absence of specific New Testament illustrations of the New England Way; he argued that in so far as "Christian" nations and princes had tried to confound civil and religious affairs, they had been failures, causing strife and persecutions.[34]

The obvious meaning of the New Testament, for Williams, was that Christ did not intend that men should be coerced in spiritual matters. Christ ordained the power of the sword, but it was given to the magistrates only to keep peace among men's bodies—to insure their physical well-being. There was a sword in the spiritual world, but it was the persuasion of the Word.[35] Thus, Williams argued for the separation of church and state.

Williams' view of persecution and liberty of conscience was a natural corollary to his argument on church and state. Persecution followed when the state invaded the sphere of spiritual matters, when magistrates interfered with a person's exercise of religion. Conscience was part of this problem in Williams' thinking, as the title of his most famous book, *The Bloody Tenet, of Persecution, for the Cause of Conscience* . . . , indicates.[36]

Conscience, wrote Williams, is "a fixed persuasion in the mind and heart of man, which enforceth him to judge (as Paul said of himself, a persecutor) and to do so and so, with respect to God, his worship, etc."[37] Williams said little else about what conscience was, for he was not concerned with an exact epistemological definition; rather, his interest centered on how conscience was a basic capacity of man, "a fixed persuasion . . . that enforceth him to judge."

Williams did not claim that conscience was without error in matters of religion.[38] In fact, it was precisely because conscience was so susceptible to error that Williams argued that it must be left at liberty in matters of religion. Thus religious truth was difficult to obtain; hence, there was little chance that religious leaders, much less civil magistrates, could isolate it. If leaders could not with much certainty state the truth, there was little chance that institutional religion, or the state, could possess the truth. Forced conformity, Williams concluded, to institutional versions of religion was likely to be an imposition of error as well as an unwarranted invasion of the individual's religious responsibility.[39]

Liberty of conscience for Williams was not based upon an optimistic view of man's ability; yet he was confident that if men were left alone to exercise their religious inclination, the ultimate cause of truth would be served. History demonstrated that when men fought wars, the cause usually was based upon religious convictions. In such cases, according to Williams, it was obvious that men's bodies could be coerced, but never their souls,[40] their inner source of religious conviction. Pursuing this view Williams concluded that the civil state had no right to interfere with Catholics, Jews, nor even Quakers, for physical punishment of the body could never reach the condition of the soul.[41]

The results of civil, or ecclesiastical, force on a person in matters of conscience were clear to Williams, and the results were all bad. Corporal punishment might "cause men to play hypocrite, and dissemble in their religion, to turn and return with the tide, as all experience in the nations of the world doth testify now."[42] It was obvious to Williams that "all false teachers and their followers" contact "a brawny and steely hardness from their sufferings for their conscience."[43] If the victim of force acquiesced and acted against his conscience, it was weakened, "since conscience to God violated, proves . . . [to be] a drug, loose and unconscionable in all converse with men."[44]

One additional aspect of Williams' view of conscience in relation to the state needs to be mentioned, that is, that the role of the state was not merely a negative one. Williams posed the question, "What is then the express duty of the civil magistrate, as to Christ Jesus, his Gospel and Kingdom?"[45] The answer turns upon "two hinges," these being observed in the two essential responsibilities of magistrates:

> First, in removing the civil bars, obstructions, hindrances, in taking of those yokes, that pinch the very souls and consciences of men, such as yet are the payments of tithe, and the maintenance of ministers. . . .
>
> Secondly, in a free and absolute permission of the consciences of all men, in what is merely spiritual, not the very consciences

of Jews, nor the consciences of the Turks or Papists, or Pagans themselves excepted.[46]

A most succinct statement of Williams' whole argument appears a few lines following; there he states, "I plead the conscience of all men to be at liberty."[47]

From the foregoing it is clear that Williams' view of conscience was radically different from that of Cotton and Ames. In contrast to them he posited liberty of conscience as a fundamental right taught by Christ in the New Testament. Williams sensed the relationship between liberty of conscience and sphere sovereignty, this being evident in his argument for a limitation on the power and authority that resided in each of these spheres. When the church or state, or both of them together, overstepped their bounds, they crushed liberty of conscience. At the same time Williams, like Perkins, recognized the spheres of church and state to have specific powers and duties. His main emphasis, however, was upon those areas where these institutions had overstepped the limits of their jurisdiction.

In conclusion, concerning Roger Williams and the Massachusetts Bay Colony, it may be said that they represented two distinctly different views of the place of conscience in the affairs of men. The colony's leaders made it clear from the beginning that they saw their experiment as one that rested upon a system of known and fixed principles, this position aptly labeled as "orthodoxy" by Perry Miller. While the question of conscience does not appear to have been central in the colony's dispute with Roger Williams before he was banished, it became a central issue subsequently. John Cotton spoke for the colony's position and from his comments on conscience it is clear that it was an expression of the Amesian view. Cotton did not speak of conscience as something that enjoyed liberty; rather liberty of conscience for him meant liberty to believe orthodoxy. This view contrasts sharply with that set forth by Williams after he left the colony. Williams argued for liberty of conscience in terms of sphere sovereignty, his view being the same as that of William Perkins.

This dispute between Massachusetts Bay Colony leaders and Roger Williams was, however, only the first conflict between the idea of toleration as developed by Ames and the claim of liberty of conscience in the tradition of William Perkins. The Antinomian Controversy of 1636-1638 also demonstrated the fundamental conflict between the Amesian view of conscience and that developed by Perkins.

B. *The Antinomian Controversy: 1636-1638*

The "most wild and desperate enthusiasm in the world" was Governor Winthrop's way of describing the antinomian party that threatened his colony in the years 1636-1638.[48] Undoubtedly Winthrop's remarks were intended for consumption in Old England, though they do evidence the degree of concern among leaders of the orthodoxy party in the Massachusetts Bay Colony. How antinomianism came to be a threat and what it meant for the problem of toleration and liberty as attitudes toward conscience is the subject of this section.

The threat of antinomianism was a different and more difficult problem for the leaders of Massachusetts Bay Colony than that of Roger Williams. The task of bringing Williams to trial and the sentence of banishment had been relatively easy. While Williams' subsequent fulminations about life in the colony and his sharp remarks about the absence of liberty of conscience were undoubtedly a source of embarrassment for the leaders, these denunciations had the virtue of coming from outside the colony itself. The antinomian problem, on the other hand, was a critique from within, and it embroiled a large number of colonists.[49]

Students of early Massachusetts Bay history differ as to the meaning of the Antinomian Controversy, but whatever else was involved, the question of dissent was prominent. Students of the problem also differ on the question of whether it was largely a dispute between a handful of people centered around Anne Hutchinson, or whether it was an issue that involved the bulk of society. From the perspective of the question of dissent Anne Hutchinson played a leading role, and the development of the controversy may profitably be traced in terms of her place in it.

While Anne Hutchinson's activities following her arrival in Massachusetts Bay in 1634 bear more directly on her place in the Antinomian Controversy, a few observations about her life in Old England will contribute to an understanding of her views. Born in 1591, she grew up under the influence of her preacher-father. Though born in Lincolnshire, she moved with her parents to London, residing there until she married William Hutchinson, a Lincolnshire merchant, the marriage precipitating a return to Lincolnshire in 1612. The return to Lincolnshire is important because in the same year a young preacher, just graduated from Cambridge, took a parish in Boston, not far from the Hutchinsons; his name was John Cotton. Soon Cotton gained a reputation as a preacher, and people came from great distances to hear him preach, including Anne Hutchinson. When Cotton left Boston, Lincolnshire, in 1633, Anne Hutchinson was greatly distressed. She had become a devotee of Cotton and felt she "could not rest" until she could again sit at the feet of her favorite preacher. The record indicates that the Hutchinsons came to Boston in New England in 1634, and some writers have suggested that they came to satisfy Anne Hutchinson's desire to again hear Cotton preach.[50] No doubt William Hutchinson wished to satisfy this desire of his wife, though he could not have overlooked the prospect of new business opportunities in the rapidly expanding colony.

Between the time of their arrival in 1634 and the outbreak of the Antinomian Controversy in 1636 the Hutchinsons established themselves in the Boston community. William was active in both business and politics, while Anne became involved in a number of activities.[51] As for church, they attended the one in which John Wilson was pastor and John Cotton, preacher.

The controversy over antinomianism was directly related to the reaction of Anne Hutchinson to the preaching of Cotton, he sharing the pulpit with John Wilson. Anne invited people to her home to discuss with them what had been said by preacher Cotton. Discussion during the week of what had been preached on the previous Sunday was not an unusual practice in the seventeenth century, but in the Hutchinson home Anne expounded vigorously what she conceived to be the essence of Cotton's views. As more people came to these meetings, on occasion as many as sixty, the inevitable occurred; Cotton's preaching was compared with that of other preachers in the Bay colony.[52]

Anne claimed that Cotton preached better doctrine than did the other preachers in the colony. She pointed out that he stressed "free grace," while the others taught a "legal scheme" of salvation.[53] In this she was commenting on a central doctrine in Reformed theology, the doctrine of justification.[54] While there was some room for differences of opinion in the interpretation of this doctrine, Anne seemed to suggest that there was, in fact, a great difference between Cotton's view and that of other preachers. Just exactly what she had in mind, just exactly what she did say to those in her home became a central point of dispute as the controversy developed. The phrase "legal scheme" of salvation could readily be interpreted as salvation by works, a view that had been contested by Reformed and other Protestants since the days of Martin Luther. Historians have had a difficult time in attempting to untangle the variety of statements and representations concerning this doctrine in the Antinomian Controversy. This difficulty undoubtedly has its basis in views stated in the controversy. Whatever it was that Anne said in her home each week captured the imagination of many people, for soon her views were spread about town.[55]

The role of Cotton in the controversy is clouded.[56] No doubt there was a difference between what he preached and what others preached, but the question as to what he did say was not easily answered. He was asked to state his view on justification on numerous occasions by other preachers. Then he was asked about other questions that were tangents to this doctrine. Finally, he was asked to write out his views to a batch of questions. Cotton responded to the private conversations; then he responded to the request that he write out his views. In each case, however, as in the formal public hearing later, Cotton answered in the only way he knew, as a scholar. His written comments on the questions submitted to him by the other preachers display the learning and technique of a skilled theologian. Throughout the controversy Cotton insisted that the differences between his views and those of the other preachers were not all that had been suggested. Cotton insisted, too, that Anne Hutchinson's views were not all that bad, until she stated in her trial, under great pressure, that she had special revelations from God.[57]

While the central issue in the controversy was Cotton's teachings and Anne Hutchinson's representations of them, the way Massachusetts Bay leaders handled Anne Hutchinson and those associated with her, those identified as antinomians, is more significant from the point of view of the conflict between the ideas of toleration and liberty of conscience. A review of the chain of events will reveal that the Massachusetts Bay system was based upon a view that included an attitude toward conscience that was no different from that held by governmental officials in Old England.

The first sign that something was wrong with the views that were associated with John Cotton and Anne Hutchinson came in the spring of 1636, when Thomas Shepard, a mainstay among the orthodox ministerium, warned Cotton that strange and erroneous opinions were emanating from members of his congregation.[58] Shepard's warning did not seem to stem the problem, for in October a group of ministers requested a meeting with Cotton, Anne Hutchinson, and her newly arrived brother-in-law, John Wheelwright.[59] The obvious purpose was to suppress deviant opinions, and the focus was on Anne Hutchinson. During the course of this meeting Cotton satisfied the other ministers, stating that "sanctification did help evidence justification."[60] In other words, works did help evidence faith, but in what way he did not say.

This occasion appeared to have resulted in a better understanding between the defenders of orthodoxy and the suspected dissenters. That this confrontation had resulted in a meeting of the minds was an illusion, for within a few weeks the Boston Church, which already had Wilson and Cotton on its ministerial staff, proposed to call John Wheelwright.[61] Winthrop suggested that this proposal was an insult to pastor Wilson, and he viewed it as evidence of how far the infectious opinions of the antinomians had progressed. Winthrop recorded in his Journal that an open quarrel was averted in the church meeting over this proposal by his insistence that it was an establishd custom that such proposals had to be unanimous.[62]

Two months later matters were worse. The ministers met again with Cotton and Anne Hutchinson, and again his position was not clear. Anne was more forward, however, suggesting that many ministers taught a covenant of works.⁶³ In a few weeks the matter erupted in the General Court when Henry Vane tendered his resignation as governor, offering as the reason his belief that God's judgment was about to come "for these differences and dissentions."⁶⁴ Vane also claimed that he had pressing business in London. More to the point, however, was the fact that he was a friend to many in the party that had formed around Anne Hutchinson. Vane changed his mind, or it was changed for him, and he decided to stay on in the governor's chair. The Court then began to debate the question of cause for the colony's troubles.

With Vane still governor and others on the Court still sympathetic to the antinomians' cause, the orthodox party, personified by Winthrop, was in a difficult position. The breadth of division in the colony was evident in the Court itself; it could come to no resolution as to the cause of trouble. The Court thus adjourned and proclaimed a fastday, to be observed in January.⁶⁵

The events of the fastday served only to deepen the division in the colony, especially a sermon preached by John Wheelwright.⁶⁶ He clarified the position of those who stood with Anne Hutchinson, and in so doing the sermon proved to be the turning point in the orthodox party's campaign to quench the antinomians. When the Court met in March, it began by fining an obscure citizen, Steven Greensmyth, for having stated that "all ministers did teach a covenant of works," Cotton and Wheelwright excepted.⁶⁷ Clearly Greensmyth had no right to an opinion that did not agree with orthodoxy. Having dispatched a minnow, the Court turned to larger prey and ordered Wheelwright to appear. They demanded an explanation for his fastday sermon. After some debate the Court judged him guilty of "contempt and sedition" for having stirred disputes in the colony.⁶⁸ It was obvious that Wheelwright was condemned because his opinion did not agree with orthodoxy.

A minority on the Court defended Wheelwright's sermon, and they were supported by a party in Boston. The latter presented a petition to the Court stating that it did not have the right to examine Wheelwright on such a question before the Church made a determination on the matter.⁶⁹ Their petition fell on deaf ears.

The main seat of the antinomian party was in Boston, the usual meeting place of the General Court. Sensing the hostility in Boston, the Court, over the objection of a minority, adjourned the March meeting of the Court until May, and designated Cambridge as the meeting place.[70] Moving the Court to Cambridge was an advantage to the orthodox party, since the next meeting involved general elections, a chance to depose antinomian sympathizers.

As the Court convened in May, Vane insisted that they take up the Wheelwright matter due to the petition having been presented on his behalf. The majority insisted, over Vane's protest, that this Court was primarily one of election, and that was the first order of business. In the election Winthrop was elected governor, while Thomas Dudley became deputy governor. Dudley had even less patience than Winthrop when it came to the antinomians.[71]

The election demonstrated that the orthodox party had support outside of Boston, and thus was in a position to deal more vigorously with the cancerous antinomian problem. Thomas Shepard preached the election sermon, and in it he reported that the differences between Cotton and the rest were slight.[72] Harmony seemed within reach, but whatever chance there was for it was washed away by one piece of legislation passed by the Court. It stated:

> It is ordered that no town or person shall receive any stranger, resorting hither with intent to reside in this jurisdiction, nor shall allow any lot or habitation to any, or entertain any such above three weeks, except such person shall have allowance under the hands of some one of the council, or of two other magistrates, upon pain that every town that shall give or sell any lot or habitation to any such, not so allowed, shall forfeit 100 pounds for every offense, and every person receiving any such, for longer than is here expressed . . . shall forfeit for every offense 40 pounds. . . .[73]

The intent of the Court's order could not be missed. It now had the power to decide who should be allowed within the colony. The effect of the order was to transfer the power to decide who was fit to live in the colony from the hands of town officials to the General Court. Heretofore each church examined persons who sought to settle near it in the colony; each church decided whom it would accept. Now the

Court would decide who was acceptable and whose opinions were acceptable. Even a person with a Christian reputation could be refused admission to the colony. Winthrop admitted as much in a letter to Vane, "A man that is a true Christian may be denied residence among us. . . ."[74] In passing this measure the Court had the means to exclude other antinomians, and anyone whose opinions they did not like. If there had been an illusion or pretense of freedom and liberty of conscience before in the colony, it vanished with this order of the Court.

Notwithstanding the fact that the election had turned over the Court almost completely into the hands of the orthodox party, and that it had passed an act restricting settlement, the theological issue in question remained in dispute. Encouraged by the Court, Bay preachers decided to meet in synod to examine the issues.[75] They met in August and listed some ninety points of doctrine that had come under fire. Most of these were dispatched without much debate. Two received special attention, the pastors concluding that the antinomians had abused the "liberty" to question ministers, and that they had improperly held "private" meetings.[76]

These conclusions reflect the prevailing attitude among orthodox preachers in the Bay colony. When they spoke of abusing "liberty" to question ministers, it would appear they meant that one had liberty to agree with the ministers, that one did not have liberty to disagree with them. Their criticism of "private" meetings appeared to be another way of saying that Bay colony citizens did not have the right to assemble and discuss deviant opinions.

The May Court and the August synod consolidated the position of the orthodox party, each demonstrating that they intended to repress or exorcise antinomians. The November Court confirmed the sense of confidence evident among the orthodox party. Methodically the Court charged numerous citizens with being antinomians, disenfranchising and banishing them.[77] Others were relieved of their "guns, pistols, swords, powder, and shot."[78] Though some of those sentenced had been involved in political action, even mob action, most were guilty of nothing more than holding unorthodox opinions.

Step by step the orthodox party was able to dissipate the strength of the antinomians, and now it was ready to proceed against Anne Hutchinson, the one they saw as the chief source of the trouble. Her case presented a special problem, since she had not been involved in any of the politics of the controversy. If they were to banish her from the colony, some means had to be devised.

The record of Anne Hutchinson's examination before the Court is pathetic from a legal standpoint.[79] The Court had nothing concrete with which to charge her; thus the proceeding rambled from one hearsay argument to another. It was only after long hours of charge and countercharge that Anne, in what could only have been an unguarded moment, stated that she had heavenly revelations in the same way that the Old Testament's Daniel did.[80] The Court seized upon this point and made short work of judging her guilty of heresy, sentencing her to banishment.

The record of Anne's examination is valuable, however, as evidence of how the orthodox party viewed liberty of conscience. Winthrop began the examination by noting that Anne had troubled the peace of the commonwealth; then he got to the heart of the matter: "You are known to be a woman that hath had a great share in the promoting and divulging of those opinions that are causes of this trouble. . . ."[81] Like the others, she was charged with holding opinions that were not acceptable in the Bay. Then Winthrop declared,

> You are . . . nearly joined not only in affinity and affection with some of those the court had taken notice of and passed censure upon, but you have spoken diverse things as we have been informed very prejudicial to the honor of the churches and ministers thereof, and you have maintained a meeting and an assembly in your house that hath been condemned by the general assembly as a thing not tolerable nor comely in the sight of God nor fitting for your sex. . . .[82]

In Winthrop's thinking she was guilty by association. He went on to state that she had been called before the Court so that it could find out whether she held the same opinions as those that had been "handled" already by the Court.

Following Winthrop's rambling statement as to why she had been brought before the Court, Anne said, "I am called here to answer before you but I hear no things laid to my charge." Winthrop insisted that he had stated charges, and she replied, "Name one, Sir." Winthrop asked whether he had not named one already, and she asked again what she had done. "You did harbour and countenance those that are parties in this faction that you have heard of," said Winthrop.[83] "That's a matter of conscience, Sir," Anne replied. "Your conscience you must keep or it must be kept for you," was his reply. "Must I not then entertain the saints because I must keep my conscience?" Anne retorted. Winthrop replied with an example:

> Say that one brother should commit felony or treason and come to his other brother's house, if he knows him guilty and conceals him he is guilty of the same. It is his conscience to entertain him, but if his conscience comes into act in giving countenance and entertainment to him that hath broken the law he is guilty too. So, if you do countenance those that are transgressors of the law you are in the same fact.

When asked what law had been broken in her having saints into her house, Winthrop cited the command to honor father and mother, and by father he meant fathers of the commonwealth.[84]

The brief dispute about the role of conscience is most revealing. Anne assumed that what went on in her house, and how she related to those charged with heresy was a question of conscience. In her mind it was a matter of personal judgment whether she held the same view they did. It was also a personal matter, a right of conscience, to agree or disagree with them. She echoed the view of William Perkins that God hath in the New Testament given a liberty to conscience.[85] She could agree, too, with Roger Williams when he said, "I plead the conscience of all men to be at liberty."[86]

Winthrop's terse reply to her claim of liberty of conscience is but a paraphrase of Ames's view of conscience. "Your conscience you must keep or it must be kept for you," was another way of saying that her conscience had to be consistent with orthodoxy or the keepers of orthodoxy would judge to what degree her conscience strayed from truth. Implied in Winthrop's statement was the idea of the "rightly informed" conscience that Ames used in his discussion of heresy. Said Ames, "When the truth is not only manifestly revealed in Scripture, but is also *sufficiently propounded*" to a person, and the person "doth so adhere to his error, that he . . . opposeth himself to the plain Scripture," he is guilty of heresy.[87] The key to the whole argument rests on the concept of a "rightly informed" conscience, the overwhelming implication being that orthodox leaders were the custodians of truth.

Late in the trial Anne again spoke of conscience. As she defended her view of Scripture and how the Holy Spirit worked, she said, "Now if you condemn me for speaking what in my conscience I know to be true I must commit myself unto the Lord."[88] Here, as in the early part of the trial, she claimed as authority her conscience over against the views of the state and church. She assumed here as before that conscience had a liberty that transcends other men and institutions. In the same passage Anne made the important distinction between power over the body and power over the soul. "You have power over my body but the Lord Jesus hath power over my body and soul."[89] The distinction between power over the body as separate from power over the soul was typical of those who stood for liberty of conscience, and this distinction was absent in a view like Winthrop's.

The difference between the concept of conscience evident in Winthrop and Anne Hutchinson was fundamental. Anne, in the tradition of William Perkins, assumed that conscience was sovereign as over against other men and institutions, while Winthrop argued that conscience was liable to the judgment and subject to the control of some human agency. This difference is not diluted by the fact that both of them readily spoke of conscience, for the evidence suggests that Winthrop did not understand Anne's appeal to conscience as sovereign. His reply to one of her questions, a reply that gave an example of a felon as coming under the authority of the state, missed the point she wanted to make. Winthrop did not see the difference between the authority of the state reaching to a felony and the authority of the state reaching an opinion held for conscience' sake. Even Ames, the master of the system of concepts that made up Massachusetts Bay orthodoxy, made a distinction between treasonous felony and heretical ideas.[90]

C. Conclusion

The manner in which Massachusetts Bay Colony leaders handled the threats posed by Roger Williams and the antinomians shows clearly that they did not intend their colony as a haven for the persecuted and oppressed, as has sometimes been suggested. On the contrary, Winthrop indicated that the leadership of the colony intended it to be an example of what the godly community should be. In his view uniformity was a keystone in the structure. The needs of the community and its purpose took precedence over all private views, whims, and interests, according to Winthrop.

The way Williams and the antinomians were treated also indicated the frame of reference within which the leaders of the orthodox party operated. Perry Miller and others have argued convincingly that the basis of orthodoxy in Massachusetts was the theology of William Ames, though Miller did not concern himself with the relationship of Ames's view of conscience to the thinking of the colony's leaders. Aware of Ames's distinctive view of conscience, one that eliminated the need to think of conscience in terms of liberty, it becomes obvious that Massachusetts Bay leaders followed William Ames in the matter of conscience as they had in other matters. Adopting the views of Ames on conscience and applying them in practice meant that the leaders of the Massachusetts Bay Colony established a policy that was no different from that which had existed among English governmental officials for generations. In the view of the colony's leaders conscience was something that came within the purview of their authority. They would decide what was an acceptable conscientious practice; they made it clear in the case of Roger Williams, and later in the Antinomian Controversy, that there was little room for deviation from the established orthodoxy. The attitude of the leaders of Massachusetts Bay had one advantage over that of English government officials; their view was rooted in a far more systematic scheme and thus was capable of a more easy application.

In terms of sphere sovereignty, the use of the Amesian view of conscience in Massachusetts Bay led to the same result as had occurred in Old England. The spheres of the church and state were

BUILDERS OF THE BAY COLONY: 1630–1640   81

expanded at the expense of individual sovereignty and liberty. This process was more exaggerated in New England, however, no doubt due to the fact that the colony began as a new venture, a venture unencumbered with the accumulated traditions that restrain an established government. The harshness of the Massachusetts Bay leaders' attitude, the narrow range of dissent that they would allow, was also supported by their belief that the church and state could be recreated according to the Mosaic example.

As the decade of the 1630's came to a close, Winthrop and his friends undoubtedly felt satisfied in the way that they had handled dissenters. Their extrication of dissent provided hope that their experiment might yet succeed. The events of the next decade in Old England —the Civil War—would illustrate, however, that the attitude of the Massachusetts Bay leaders toward conscience was not the wave of the future, as Winthrop thought; rather, it was a mere ripple in the wave of the past.

CHAPTER NOTES

1. Quoted in Lawrence Leder, *Liberty and Authority* (Chicago, 1968), p. 62.
2. *Ibid.*
3. *Ibid.*
4. Perry Miller and Thomas H. Johnson, eds., *The Puritans: A Sourcebook of Their Writings* (New York, 1938), p. 195.
5. *Ibid.*, p. 197.
6. Miller, *Orthodoxy*, chap. VI.
7. *Supra*, p. 38.
8. *The Complete Writings of Roger Williams* (New York, 1963); hereinafter cited as Williams, *Works*. This is a reprint of the Narragansett edition with a seventh volume added under the direction of Perry Miller. The seventh volume contains an essay by Miller and a number of items written by Williams that have come to light since the Narragansett edition was published in the nineteenth century.
9. *Ibid.*, p. 6.
10. Samuel H. Brockunier, *The Irrepressible Democrat: Roger Williams* (New York, 1940), and Vernon L. Parrington, *The Colonial Mind* (New York, 1927), p. 62 ff.
11. Perry Miller, *Roger Williams: His Contribution to the American Tradition* (New York, 1962), comments on this problem, pp. v, 27, 28, 254.

12. Miller, *Roger Williams*, p. 43 ff.; see also Larzer Ziff, *The Career of John Cotton* (Princeton, 1962), p. 85 ff.; hereinafter cited as Ziff, *Cotton Career*.
13. Williams, *Works*, VII, p. 7.
14. *Ibid.*
15. Ziff, *Cotton Career*, p. 88.
16. *Ibid.*
17. Williams, *Works*, VII, pp. 7-8.
18. James K. Hosmer, ed., *Winthrop's Journal* (New York, 1908), I, pp.162-163; hereinafter cited as Winthrop, *Journal*.
19. Williams, *Works*, VII, p. 8. See also the same view in his *Roger Williams*, p. 37 ff.
20. Joseph Rosenmeier, "The Teacher and the Witness: John Cotton and Roger Williams," *William and Mary Quarterly*, Series 3, XXV (July, 1968), pp. 408-431.
21. Sacvan Bercovitch, "Typology in Puritan New England: The Williams-Cotton Controversy Reassessed," *American Quarterly*, XIX (Summer, 1967), pp. 166-191.
22. The arguments of Rosenmeier and Bercovitch, noted above, raise many questions about the interpretation of Puritanism, resolution of them falling outside the scope of this study. Rosenmeier, for example, suggests that the central issue between Williams and Cotton was a question of the meaning of the incarnation, and that the typological problem was a function of this issue. While his point about the place of the incarnation in the controversy serves as useful information, his sub-joining the typological problem to it is questionable. More important, however, is the fact that his discussion of the place of the incarnation in the controversy, together with Bercovitch's point about typology, suggests that in time a major realignment of the interpretation of Puritanism may be in order. This direction of Puritan studies seems to be supported by a growing appreciation of fundamental differences between leading figures, the difference between Perkins and Ames suggested in this study being an example.
23. Williams, *Works*, contains writings of John Cotton in addition to those of Williams. Larzer Ziff has edited additional works of Cotton published as *John Cotton on the Churches of New England* (Cambridge, 1968); hereinafter cited as Ziff, *Cotton Church*.
24. *Ibid.*
25. Ziff, *Cotton Career*, p. 85 ff.
26. *Ibid.*, p. 92.
27. Williams, *Works*, III, p. 42 ff.
28. *Ibid.*
29. *Ibid.*, p. 92.
30. Ames, *Conscience*, bk. 4, p. 11.

31. The *Bloody Tenet* was published in 1644.
32. Williams, *Works*, VII, p. 21.
33. *Ibid.*, I, p. 112.
34. *Ibid.*, III, p. 181; see also pp. 248-249.
35. *Ibid.*, III, p. 181, and VII, p. 179.
36. *Ibid.*, III, p. 181 ff.
37. *Ibid.*, IV, p. 508.
38. Edmund S. Morgan, *Roger Williams: The Church and the State* (New York, 1967), p. 135.
39. This is the main thrust of the *Bloody Tenet*.
40. Williams, *Works*, VII, p. 179 ff.
41. *Ibid.*, IV, pp. 506-507.
42. *Ibid.*, p. 209.
43. *Ibid.*, III, p. 272.
44. *Ibid.*, p. 498.
45. *Ibid.*, VII, p. 178.
46. *Ibid.*
47. *Ibid.*, p. 179.
48. Quoted in Ziff, *Cotton Career*, p. 140.
49. The events described here are based upon Ziff, *Cotton Career*, chap. IV; David D. Hall, ed., *The Antinomian Controversy, 1636-1638* (Middletown, Conn., 1968), hereinafter cited as Hall, *A.C.*; and relevant passages in Winthrop, *Journal*.
50. Hall, *A.C.*, p. 5.
51. *Ibid.*
52. *Ibid.*
53. *Ibid.*
54. It is interesting to note that for Calvin the idea of justification was relatively simple, this contrasting to the increasingly complicated statement of the doctrine among Puritans. See the subject in *The New Schaff-Herzog Encyclopedia of Religious Knowledge* (Grand Rapids, 1950).
55. Hall, *A.C.*, p. 7.
56. Hall is less sympathetic toward Cotton than Ziff.
57. Hall, *A.C.*, p. 7.
58. *Ibid.*
59. *Ibid.*
60. *Ibid.*, p. 6.
61. *Ibid.*
62. *Ibid.*
63. *Ibid.*, p. 7.
64. *Ibid.*
65. *Ibid.*
66. *Ibid.*

67. Ziff, *Cotton Career*, pp. 125-126.
68. Hall, *A.C.*, p. 8.
69. For a detailed discussion of the church's examination of Mrs. Hutchinson, see Ziff, *Cotton Career*, p. 143 ff.
70. Hall, *A.C.*, p. 8. Cambridge was at that time known as Newton.
71. *Ibid.*
72. Thomas Shepard was a leading figure in the Massachusetts Bay Colony. There has been no modern study of him, to my knowledge. His writings, available as *The Works of Thomas Shepard* (Boston, 1853, reprinted in New York, 1967), are a classic example of the typical "orthodox" divine in the early period of Massachusetts Bay history.
73. For a discussion of the place of legislation in the colony, see Hall, *A.C.*, p. 251, n. 40. The order of the court appears in *Massachusetts Records*, I, p. 196.
74. John Winthrop, "A Defense of an Order of the Court Made in the Year 1637," *Publications of the Prince Society*, I, p. 82.
75. Hall, *A.C.*, p. 8. The errors of the antinomian party are found in Winthrop's account, published as chap. VIII in Hall, *A.C.*
76. Hall, *A.C.*, p. 8.
77. *Ibid.*
78. *Ibid.*
79. The text of "The Examination of Mrs. Hutchinson at the Court at Newton" may be found in Hall, *A.C.*, chap. IX. For a discussion of the legal aspects of the trial, or hearing, see George Lee Haskins, *Law and Authority in Early Massachusetts* (New York, 1960), pp. 49-51.
80. Hall, *A.C.*, p. 337.
81. *Ibid.*, p. 312.
82. *Ibid.*
83. *Ibid.*
84. *Ibid.*, pp. 312-313.
85. *Supra*, p. 4.
86. *Supra*, p. 69.
87. *Supra*, p. 65 (italics mine).
88. Hall, *A.C.*, p. 337.
89. *Ibid.*, p. 338.
90. *Supra*, p. 50.

Chapter IV

LIBERTY OF CONSCIENCE IN OLD ENGLAND
1640-1660

The decades between the convention of the Long Parliament in 1640 and the Restoration of the Crown in 1660 were crucial in the history of the conflict between the policy of toleration and the claim of liberty of conscience. It was the time when the claim of liberty moved from a stage of gestation in English thought to that of birth, a time when it became a central theme in numerous and powerful factions in politics and religion, and a time when it boldly challenged the firmly entrenched doctrine of governmental toleration. During the brief period of Cromwell and his friends, governmental toleration gave way to a recognition of the rights of conscience and its liberty as the notion reached a broad popularized level. Though this triumph was brief, English political and religious thought was never again the same.

In a broad perspective, the significance of liberty of conscience in the Civil War era stems from the fact that the social upheaval of the period brought into the open those people and factions in English society who saw merit in the argument for liberty of conscience. Though liberty of conscience was not the central issue in the Civil War, it was a prominent factor because it was embraced by numerous factions and because it could be used to support a broad range of programs. For example, as will be evident, liberty of conscience could be embraced by both presbyterians and independents, though these groups differed sharply on other issues. As a result of the popularization of liberty of conscience during the Civil War, the idea became a creed in the years to come, and it could not be vanquished, not even under the restored monarchy.

A. *Liberty and Sovereignty in the Westminster Assembly*

That the idea of liberty of conscience ended its gestation, that it came of age in the Civil War, is most obvious in the Westminster Assembly. The one problem plaguing Parliament long before it convened in 1640 had been the church question. It was natural, therefore, that soon after convening, the Long Parliament issued an ordinance calling for "an assembly of learned and godly divines."[1] A list of delegates was drawn up,[2] and in time they met at the place from which the assembly took its name.

The parliamentary ordinance calling the assembly also spelled out what its task was:

> To be consulted with by Parliament, for the settling of the government and liturgy of the Church of England, and for vindicating and clearing the doctrine of said church from false aspersions and interpretations.[3]

More specifically, the ordinance charged the assembly with creating a government for the church "as may be most agreeable to God's Holy Word."[4] The Westminster Assembly was called thus to settle that question that had for so long remained unresolved in England.

The assembly gathered in the spring of 1643 and considered the church question, as well as many other points of doctrine, stating its conclusions in its Confession of Faith and in other documents. In the Confession the assembly wrote the following comment on conscience, words that are strikingly similar to those of William Perkins:

> God alone is Lord of the conscience, and hath left it free from the doctrines and commandments of men which are in any thing contrary to his Word, or beside it, in matters of faith or worship. So that to believe such doctrines or obey such commandments out of conscience is to betray true liberty of conscience; and the requiring of an implicit faith, and an absolute and blind obedience, is to destroy liberty of conscience, and reason also.[5]

The Westminster Assembly, therefore, became the first Reformation council to make a confessional statement on liberty of conscience. In terms of the English Reformation, the claim of liberty of conscience, made so often since the days of William Perkins, now became part of the creedal baggage of the English Church.[6]

While it was an achievement for the assembly to state its belief in liberty of conscience, the confessional statement alone did not account for the full significance of the idea of the assembly's work. The statement on conscience in the Confession was, in fact, part of the assembly's resolution of the church question, and only as part of that problem can the assembly's view of conscience be appreciated.

The church question in the assembly consisted of two closely linked parts, one being the church-state dispute, the other, the presbyterian-independency dispute. Distinguishing between the two facets of the church question is vital, because historically they have been confused. In a broad perspective the assembly's contribution to the resolution of the first is more important than what it had to say about the second. Concern here involves the assembly's answer to the query, whether or not the church should be separated from the state. This is always to be separated from the second question, namely, whether the institutional form of the church should be presbyterian or congregational.[7]

Contemporaries spoke of the church-state dispute as the Erastian controversy. Erastians in the English Civil War era, like the earlier followers of the sixteenth-century theologian Thomas Erastus, advocated a system in which the church was subordinated to the state.[8] Of course, the Elizabethan Church was an arm of the state, but reform-minded protestants usually objected to this arrangement. The label "Erastian" in the reforming climate of the Civil War was attached to a party of protestants who were interested in reform, but not in the separation of church and state.[9] It was a term used with bitter feeling, because it carried with it a feeling of betrayal of the potential of church reform. Parliament as usurper or successor to royal power predictably lodged a large contingent of Erastians. They might support a national presbyterian church, but it would still, in their view, be a creature of the state.

Parliamentary Erastians drew upon the tradition of politics and the tradition of religion to support their contention that the church was, or should be, a creature of the state. Parliamentary lawyers, steeped in the history of Roman law, saw the separated church as a violation of the time-honored maxim *imperium in imperio*, as a republic within a republic. Others defended the Erastian position by appeal to the Mosaic example, a view that saw the Old Testament practice as normative for the Christian church.[10]

While the Westminster Assembly's members were almost all opposed to the Erastian position, four or five of them were Erastians. The leader of this small band was John Seldon, perhaps the outstanding Hebrew scholar of the century. The assembly's protocol called for the free expression of all views;[11] hence, Seldon had a chance to present his arguments as the church question came to debate. Seldon's defense of a state church was a long and learned oration. Reports of it suggest that it was a model of scholastic learning, a real tribute in a scholastic age. This event has been preserved in the records of great orators, but not so much for what Seldon said as for what was said by another after he sat down. Legend has it that Seldon left his audience breathless, for no one could possibly refute him. Surprise, amazement, and then admiration filled the assembly's chambers as a young scholar stood, refuting every point made by Seldon. Without notes, without preparation, the legend claims, George Gillespie vanquished the Erastian argument of its greatest proponent.[12]

The David and Goliath aspects of this debate undoubtedly grew up around the story, but it was important because it focused on the fact that the Parliament and the assembly held positions that could not be reconciled. There could be no compromise; either the church was separate or it was a creature of the state.

The assembly's view of the church could not be reconciled with the wishes of Parliament because it was rooted in the idea of sphere sovereignty, a stance that had profound implications for the problem of conscience. Concerning the sphere of the church the assembly wrote, "There is no other Head of the Church, but the Lord Jesus Christ."[13] Of course, the Erastian could agree with this if he added the qualification that Christ, as Head of the church, had delegated authority to magistrates to care for the church. That was not, however, what the assembly had in mind, for the Divines also stated "that Jesus as King and Head of His Church hath appointed an ecclesiastical government in His Church in the hands of Church Officers distinct from civil government."[14] The sphere of the church was not only distinct, it was also limited, a point the assembly made when it stated:

> Synods and councils are to handle or conclude nothing but that which is ecclesiastical, and are not to intermeddle with civil affairs which concern the commonwealth, unless by way of humble petition in cases extraordinary; or by way of advice for satisfaction of conscience, if they be thereunto required by the civil magistrate.[15]

If the church was a distinct and separate sphere, it naturally followed that the civil government was also an ordained entity. The assembly affirmed this position in its usual pithy language. Of magistrates, the Divines wrote:

> God, the Supreme Lord and King of all the world, hath ordained civil magistrates to be under him over the people, for his own glory and the public good; and, to this end, hath armed them with the power of the sword, for the defense and encouragement of them that are good and for the punishment of evildoers.[16]

Stressing the limits of civil sovereignty, the assembly stated, "The Civil Magistrate may not assume to himself the administration of the Word and Sacraments, or the power of the Keys of the Kingdom of Heaven."[17]

The assembly's comments regarding the proper domains of the church and of the state seem to suggest that between them was an insurmountable wall of separation.[18] Such a view would be a misreading of their intent, and a view inconsistent with the idea of sphere sovereignty. Institutions, such as the church and the state, have areas of common interest, and they have points at which they overlap. Recognizing this feature of sphere sovereignty, the assembly spelled out how the church and the state should bridge their institutional differences, how they should pursue their common interests. Quoted already was the assembly's belief that the church could petition the government in certain "extraordinary" cases, or in satisfaction of conscience.[19] At the same time the civil magistrate had the authority, even duty, to call synods if he felt that it would help keep peace in the church. The magistrate in so doing had no special license, for all had to be "according to the mind of God."[20]

In the assembly's view, God had ordained the state for specific ends, and he had done the same for the church. Each was a distinct institution, though in certain instances they were bound to help each other. Such an image of the assembly's view of society and its institutions is, however, incomplete. Separation of church and state is only part of the assembly's theory of sphere sovereignty. As heirs of the English Reformed tradition, the assembly was bound to relate the sovereignty of the institutional church and state to man, to men as individuals.[21] As Reformed Christians they knew that man was not made for the sabbath, rather the sabbath for man, and they knew that man was not made for the state, rather the state for man. A description of the powers ordained to the state and to the church would, therefore, be of little value unless the rights and liberties of the individual were recognized.

In this context the assembly's statement on conscience is more than a concession or mere acknowledgement of the role of conscience in the affairs of men. Conscience functions, rather, as an essential and integral part of the assembly's resolution of the church question. The doctrine of conscience is but another way to state the case for the sovereignty of the individual, and thus it reinforces the limits of power inherent in the church and state. The assembly's view of conscience prevents the individual from becoming a victim of double tyranny, tyranny by the church as well as by the state.

Another look at the assembly's statement on conscience, from the perspective of sovereignty, will clarify the place of conscience in the assembly's resolution of the church question. Liberty of conscience is a Christian birthright, because it is part of "the liberty which Christ hath purchased for believers under the gospel,"[22] a statement reminiscent of Perkins' contention that "Christ hath in the New Testament given a liberty to the conscience."[23] The rights of conscience are thus of the same order as the powers ordained to the state and to the church, a point emphasized by the Confession's phrase, "God alone is Lord of the conscience."[24]

The question immediately arises as to the limits of that liberty which Christ gave to conscience. The answer, in the assembly's view, hinges on the way the ordained powers of the state, the church, and the individual relate to each other. The simple fact that each of these factors has inherent, ordained rights, duties, and powers implies certain limits, for where the powers of one begin, the powers of the others must end. Once this point is understood, it becomes clear that the question of limits of power and liberty involves a defining of the liberties and duties that the state, the church, and the individual possess.

Noted already was the fact that the assembly saw state sovereignty limited to keeping the peace, encouraging good, and punishing evildoers. This point was reinforced in the Confession's claim that conscience was at liberty in relation to "the doctrines and commandments of men which are in any thing contrary to his Word, or beside it."[25] Of course, men had to obey doctrines and commandments that were enjoined by "his Word." This was another way of stating that liberty of conscience was not license, that liberty had to be consistent with the other sovereign spheres, with the powers of the state and of the church.

In the assembly's view, the exercise of liberty of conscience by the individual in relation to the powers of the state and church was not an option that one might exercise, but rather a duty. Referring to the rules of men, the Confession stated, "So that to believe such doctrines or obey such commandments out of conscience, is to betray true liberty of conscience."[26] Obeying the whims and wishes of men had to be distinguished from obeying lawful, that is, biblical commands.

Officers of the state and the church disrupted the power and place of conscience when they demanded obedience in those things that were not according to the mind of God, in those things that were contrary to the Word, or beside. Magistrates and churchmen had to restrain their desires and live within their powers because "the requiring of an implicit faith [by churchmen] and an absolute and blind obedience [by magistrates], is to destroy liberty of conscience," and, the Confession adds significantly, "reason also."[27]

The assembly thus marked off the conscience of man as a separate sovereign sphere, and it did so as part of its resolution of the issue for which it had been convened. Parliament assembled the Divines, asking them to settle the government and doctrine of the church, only to have the Divines tell them that the church, the state, and man were separately ordained creations. Each was independently responsible to God for the authority and liberty granted to it by Him. The assembly's resolution of the church question had a double-barrelled effect; on the one hand, it solved the church question, and, on the other, its conclusions were stated in the form of doctrine. In the hands of the assembly liberty of conscience became an essential doctrine, and at the same time an integral part of its view of the church.

Further evidence of the fact that the idea of liberty of conscience came of age in the Civil War era may be found in the specific writings of the assembly's Divines. Representative comments on conscience follow:

> To do God and ourselves right, it is necessary that we should with our utmost strength maintain the doctrine and power of that liberty with which Christ hath endowed His church, without . . . subjecting ourselves to their [magistrates'] servitude: so as to surrender either judgment or consciences to be wholly disposed according to the opinions or wills of men. . . .
> Thomas Taylor

> There is no power on earth, that can properly and immediately reach the conscience of men. Conscience is a thing out of men's jurisdiction, it will neither be beholden to man for its liberty, nor is it capable of his restraints, it is out of reach of all human power.
> Samuel Bolton

> There cannot be imagined a higher contempt of God than for a man to despise the power of his own conscience which is the highest sovereignty under heaven, as being God's most immediate deputy for the ordering of his life and ways.
> Robert Saunderson

> Conscience is considered by Divines as a principle of our acting in order that we do what God commanded in the Law and Gospel.
> Samuel Rutherford

> Conscience is a man's judgment of himself, of his estates and actions, as they are subjected unto the judgment of God. . . . Conscience is placed in the middle, under God and above man.
> Henry Wilkinson

> Now conscience is the spring of practice, and the wheel that must set all the rest going. . . . Conscience is a noble and divine power

planted of God in the soul, working upon itself by reflection.
... God hath given it more force and power to work upon men,
than all other agents: it being internal and domestic, hath the advantage of all foreign and outward.   Samuel Ward

As in the case of the Confession, these expressions[28] embody all the elements essential in Perkins' view of liberty of conscience, including the sphere sovereignty concept.

Like Roger Williams and others during the early Stuart period, assembly Divines often used liberty of conscience as a defense for some position taken during the Civil War era. Typical of this use of the idea appears in *An Apologetical Narration*, written in 1643.[29] This brief tract was written by five members of the Westminster Assembly, explaining how they practiced religion while in exile. The work is often cited by students of church history as evidence of a congregational view of polity. Aside from the polity question the *Apologetical Narration* is of interest because it rests its case upon liberty of conscience.

The authors in introductory remarks stated that they had, on the average, served ten years in English churches before they resolved to leave.[30] They gave their reason for leaving:

> The sinful evil of those corruptions in the public worship and government of this Church, which all do now so generally acknowledge and decry. . . .[31]

These corruptions in worship and government, they said, "took hold upon our consciences long before some other of our brethren."[32] They were not being overly scrupulous, because the evils of worship and church government "have been the common stumbling block and offense of many thousands of tender consciences."[33] Interestingly, they argued that the offenses mentioned had been afflicting tender consciences "ever since the first Reformation of Religion,"[34] that is, since the days of Queen Elizabeth.

Unwilling to submit to the evil practices set down by church leaders, unable to because these practices were doctrines and commandments of men, the authors of the *Narration* resolved to leave England. Free of the evil practices of the Church of England, the apologists resolved to inquire what church practice ought to be in terms of apostolic direction and primitive practice found in the New Testament. While this task was great, it was not impossible, because they were "to be guided by that light and touch [torch?], God's Spirit; [it] should by the Word vouchsafe our consciences, as the needle touched with the loadstone is in the compass."[35] In determining the church government most consistent with the New Testament the apologists placed conscience in a central role because, they stated:

> We had (of all men) the greatest reason to be true to our own consciences in what we should embrace, seeing it was for our consciences that we were deprived at once of what ever was dear to us.[36]

Like Perkins, and like the Confession, conscience was normative for them:

> Consciences were [so] possessed with that reverence and adoration of the fulness of the Scriptures, that there is therein a complete sufficiency, as to make the man of God perfect, so also to make the Churches of God perfect. . . .[37]

In a word, the authors of the *Apologetical Narration* presented their views on polity because they could not remain silent, for silence would have been a betrayal of "true liberty of conscience," something they could not do as members of the Westminster Assembly.

From the foregoing it is clear that the Westminster Assembly contributed to the spread of the claim of liberty of conscience during the Civil War era. The assembly's Confession shows clearly that the Divines were committed to the idea of sphere sovereignty, that it was part of their view of the liberty that God had given to conscience. Individual members of the assembly also used liberty of conscience in terms of sphere sovereignty to defend particular positions they held, an example being the authors of the *Apologetical Narration*. Collectively and individually, the assembly embraced liberty of conscience in the way that it had been stated a half-century earlier by William Perkins.

The Divines of the assembly were not the only ones during the Civil War who expressed their adherence to the concept of conscience and its liberty through sphere sovereignty, for it was also prominent in the Leveller movement.

B. Liberty of Conscience and the Leveller Movement

The word *Leveller*, like the word *Puritan*, was first used in derision. It came into being after the movement it described.[38] Historically the term applied to a faction in the English Civil War that advocated a series of reforms aimed at expanding the rights of all citizens. As the term suggests, the proposed reforms would equalize classes and people; at least they would all be on one level before the law. This has been described as a democratic movement, as the precursor to modern democracy. Modern writers have, therefore, extolled the virtues and programs of the Leveller party.[39]

Debates about the origin and scope of the Leveller movement continue, but these debates do not alter the fact that a number of the party called Levellers played significant roles in the shaping of Civil War reforms. Like the Westminster Confession, like many of the assembly's Divines, Levellers posited liberty of conscience as an essential element in the solution of the acrimonious and factious disputes of the Civil War. As the foremost student of the Leveller movement, T. C. Pease, has said, liberty of conscience "was a fundamental article in the creed of the Levellers."[40]

The Leveller movement was essentially a layman's political movement; thus its interest in the rights of conscience adds another dimension to that theologically oriented one of the Westminster Assembly. Though a considerable number of Levellers wrote on the place of liberty of conscience in the reformation of English society, their thinking may be sampled by an examination of the writings of three leaders—William Walwyn, Henry Robinson, and Richard Overton.

Typical of Leveller tracts on liberty of conscience was William Walwyn's *The Compassionate Samaritan*, published in 1644. The short title does not do justice to what Walwyn had in mind. The remainder of the title reads:

> Unbinding the conscience, and pouring oil into the wounds which have been made upon the separation: recommending their future welfare to the serious thoughts, and careful endeavors of all who love the peace and unity of Commonwealth's men, or desire the unanimous prosecution of the Common Enemies, or who follow

our Savior's rule, to do unto others, what they would have others do unto them.[41]

This, the full title, reveals some important clues to the nature of Walwyn's thinking. Separatists suffered because their consciences were restrained, and he wished that they be loosed. No anarchist, he seeks the peace and unity of the nation. No secular thinker, he wants men to follow the rule of Christ.

A look at the content of the document reveals that Walwyn is trying to define the limits of Christian liberty and liberty of conscience. Addressing the Commons, whom he saw as the only persons left "to play the good Samaritan's part," Walwyn expressed his belief that they would consider "the oppressed conscience" of the separatists as they continued "the Reformation so happily begun."[42] That Walwyn was attempting to define the limits of liberty appears in his first chapter, "Liberty of Conscience Asserted, and the Separatist Vindicated."[43] Walwyn had heard about *An Apologetical Narration*, he said, and "did with gladness of heart undertake the reading thereof."[44] His joy turned to sorrow, however, because the authors claimed liberty of conscience for themselves, but not for everyone. Walwyn resolved, therefore, to set down the reasons why liberty of conscience should not be limited, why it was a right of the Separatists as well.

His argument has all the marks found in the views of the assembly's Confession, in the writings of the Divines, and in the *Narration*, the only difference being in the wider application of the idea of liberty of conscience. Like the apologists of the *Narration*, Walwyn wrote his treatise as a matter of conscience. On this he said, "Me thinks every man is bound in conscience to speak and do what he can in behalf of others."[45] Walwyn wrote on behalf of the Separatists as a matter of conscience though "I myself am none."[46] That liberty of conscience was not license appears in a most succinct statement of his case:

> Now because little can be done in their behalf, unless liberty of conscience be allowed for every man, or sort of men to worship God in that way, and perform Christ's Ordinances in that manner as shall appear to them most agreeable to God's Word, and no man be punished . . . by authority for his opinions, unless it be

dangerous to the State . . . every man ought to have liberty of conscience of what opinion soever, with the caution above named. . . .[47]

Walwyn linked reason to conscience in the same way Perkins and the Divines of the assembly. "Liberty of conscience is to be allowed every man . . . because of what judgment soever a man is, he cannot choose but be of that judgment."[48] Again, "Whatsoever a man's reason doth conclude to be true or false, to be agreeable or disagreeable to God's Word," the same "to that man is his opinion or judgment."[49] Walwyn did not mean to imply that reason was likely to be correct, only that it was compelling. As for the rightness of reason, he echoed Roger Williams when he wrote, "No man, nor no sort of men can presume of an unerring spirit," because of "the uncertainty of knowledge in his life."[50]

Like other Perkinsian expressions on liberty of conscience, Walwyn's argument reflects a deep commitment to biblical principles. Linking conscience to the well-known phrase of St. Paul that "whatsoever is not of faith is sin," Walwyn wrote:

> The third reason for liberty of conscience is grounded upon these foundations, that whatsoever is not of faith is sin . . . to compel me against my conscience, is to compel me against what I believe to be true, and so against my faith: now whatsoever is not of faith is sin; to compel me therefore against my conscience, is to compel me to do that which is sinful. . . .[51]

In short, absence of liberty of conscience causes men to sin.

Like Walwyn's work, a second Leveller tract, Henry Robinson's *Liberty of Conscience*, stated its purpose in the full title:

> Liberty of Conscience: or the sole means to obtain Peace and Truth. Not only reconciling His Majesty with His subjects, but all Christians, States, and Princes to one another, with the freest passage for the Gospel. Very seasonable and necessary in these distracted times, when most men weary of war, and cannot find the way to peace.[52]

Like Walwyn, he argued that the polarity between the king's party and Parliament, and other factious disputes could be settled only when all recognized liberty of conscience.

98 LIBERTY OF CONSCIENCE

A third Leveller tract on liberty of conscience was Richard Overton's *The Arraignment of Mr. Persecution*, written in 1645. It was a brilliant piece of satire, and thus difficult to summarize.[53] Briefly, it consisted of a mock trial, all the elements that troubled English society being assigned a place in the proceedings. On the one side Overton placed all that was evil—rude-multitude, Scotch-government, false-prophets, Sir John Presbyter, Pontifical-revenue, and others. Supporting them as witnesses were Satan, Antichrist, Spanish-Inquisition, Council of Trent, High Commission, and many more. Together all these presented the case for Mr. Persecution, claiming that he had been falsely charged.

On the other side Overton placed Mr. God's Vengence to serve as prosecutor, Vengence charging Persecution with crimes against Christian, Martyr, and Liberty of Conscience. The star witness for the prosecution was none other than Sovereign Christ. The opening speech of Sovereign Christ reflects much about Overton's view of conscience:

> Gentlemen, our Lord of Lords, King of Kings, whose image and express prerogative I am, hath by the price of his blood, constituted himself sole Head and King for ever over the consciences of men. . . .[54]

This is but another way of stating what the Westminster Confession said, that is, "God alone is Lord of the conscience." That God intended conscience to be at liberty Overton expressed in the next phrases:

> Therefore he chargeth his Householders, the Kings of the earth, to let the tares and the wheat grow together in the field of the world until the harvest, the Day of Judgment.[55]

Overton here borrows a favorite parable of advocates of liberty of conscience. The implication is that the good and bad must exist side by side until the Lord of conscience comes to judge what men have done with their liberty.

Having stated the case for liberty of conscience, Sovereign Christ concludes by charging Persecution with a violation of liberty of conscience:

> Therefore the malefactor, Persecution, in my judgment, being

in his inclinations and actions altogether adverse thereto, is an Arch-traitor to the prerogative Royal of Jesus Christ over the consciences of men, and therefore lawfully and justly charged with this bill.[56]

Following these remarks by Sovereign Christ is a patient rehearsal of the many situations in which Persecution violated liberty of conscience. Overton's use of satire in *The Arraignment of Mr. Persecution* effectively conveys his belief that persecution can be avoided in the future if men would only heed the God-ordained right of liberty of conscience, a right granted to everyone.

Other Levellers, such as John Lilburne,[57] wrote on liberty of conscience, but their works need not be reviewed here. The items cited show that liberty of conscience was basic in their thought as they contemplated ways to end civil strife. These works also make it abundantly clear that their view of liberty of conscience was rooted in the same perspective found in the Westminster Confession, and among the Divines. Although a writer such as William Walwyn could criticize the *Apologetical Narration*, his criticism must be understood in terms of the problem of the limits of liberty, not as a fundamental fissure. The Leveller view of liberty of conscience, being part of the Perkinsian tradition, was a powerful argument in their drive to circumscribe royal sovereignty.

C. *Liberty of Conscience and the Policies of the Protectorate*

The execution of the king, in 1649, was a decisive event in the Civil War. From 1640 until his death any settlement of the issues would have had to take into account the king as person and the king as office. Some compromise would have to be made on the question of royal versus parliamentary power and on the church question. The Westminster Assembly, its Divines, the Levellers, and others in writing on liberty of conscience in this period assumed the existence of the monarchy, and projected liberty of conscience as a right over against it. While the king lived, while there was the prospect of a compromise settlement of the war that would include a circumscribed monarchy, the claim of liberty of conscience did not have a bright future.

With the execution of the king in 1649, the political climate experienced a fundamental change. The execution of the king was as much a death blow to the institution as it was to the person; at least this was the attitude of those in control of the government. From the point of view of the conflict between the royal policy of toleration and the claim of liberty of conscience as a right, the execution of the king signaled a new day. Of course, the future of the claim of liberty of conscience would depend upon the nature of the government that replaced the monarchy.

Those responsible for the execution of the king had plans for a republican government,[58] and with the execution there was no turning back from the move toward a republic. Establishment of a republic would be no easy task, for public opinion did not favor the idea, nor was there unanimity among those in a position to bring about the republic. Continued fighting on the domestic scene coupled with foreign battles precluded an early consolidation of republican interests.

By 1651, however, it became clear that Oliver Cromwell was at the center of power by accident or by design, or, as Cromwell himself thought, by the providence of God.[59] That Cromwell was the central figure on the political scene after 1651 did not immediately register with the members of that remnant of Parliament called the Rump.[60] They argued with him and his advisors for months, blocking his plans and suggestions until one day in April, 1653, Cromwell took a small guard with him to the House and physically ejected its members.

In place of the Rump Parliament, Cromwell and the Council of the Army installed what is known as the Barebones Parliament, a group of one hundred and forty men selected from a list drawn up by a number of congregational churches. This Parliament was supposed to legislate as well as superintend the government. Late in 1653 a new constitution called the Instrument of Government was drawn up; it provided that Cromwell be designated Lord Protector, and that he be assisted by a Council of State. As Cromwell took office, the Barebones Parliament was dissolved, and Cromwell was, to all intents and purposes, the government of England.[61]

The ascendance of Cromwell filled the political vacuum created by the execution of the king,[62] but the question of religion, and thus the question of the claim of liberty of conscience, remained unresolved. What place liberty of conscience would have in the republic depended to a large degree on Cromwell.

It can be stated categorically that Oliver Cromwell supported and defended liberty of conscience, that in his view it was an essential right in the same sense that it was for Perkins, the Divines of the assembly, the Levellers, and others during the Civil War period. To state that Cromwell defended liberty of conscience, however, probably grates upon the usual historical images of him, for he is often pictured as a fanatical dictator. For example, the most recent and perhaps the definitive collection of Cromwell's papers, collected and edited by Professor W. C. Abbott in the 1930's and 1940's, pictures Cromwell as a dictator in the mold of Hitler and other modern autocrats. The clue to Abbott's image of Cromwell, however, rests in his view of his own age, in his increasing apprehensions about the portents of a Hitler, more than it does in his analysis of Cromwell as a Christian statesman of the seventeenth century. Abbott was not the only modern historian to deal harshly with Cromwell, but his work reinforces the negative opinions of others.[63]

That Abbott saw Cromwell as a precursor to the modern dictator, that Cromwell deserves a better image, are observations made by a most perceptive student of Cromwell and the Civil War era, Robert S. Paul. True though the fact is that Cromwell led armies and ordered the execution of his enemies, that is only part of the story, as Professor Paul points out in his study, *The Lord Protector*.[64] A more accurate picture of Cromwell would stress the fact that he was a man with a vision, a Christian man with a vision of a Christian commonwealth. Cromwell's commonwealth included provisions for liberty of conscience, a stance not likely to be assumed by a Nazi dictator.

Cromwell's defense of liberty of conscience was evident in his own comments. He, like his contemporaries, was more involved with the definition of the limits of liberty of conscience than with its roots or source. As a political leader he was distressed when exercise of liberty of conscience led to civil disturbances and violences. Cromwell drew the line when liberty led to violence, but in so doing he agonized in ambivalence. Professor Paul captured the essence of this problem when he wrote:

> If Cromwell disliked persecuting those from whom he most of all dissented, he was completely embarrassed by the measures he was forced to adopt against Fifth Monarchists and Quakers, for they were men with whom he had a great deal in common.[65]

Cromwell, like Monarchists, passionately desired the coming of the kingdom of Christ. The Quaker inner light, moreover, was something Cromwell could understand. Still, wrote Professor Paul,

> He could not allow the civil disturbances caused by George Fox's followers, and between Cromwell's methods of orderly government and the Fifth Monarchists' violent and fanatical ideal of a godly oligarchy, there could be no compromise.[66]

In short, Cromwell was a reformer, but he could not abide violence.

That Cromwell saw liberty of conscience as a right, but a right that did not condone violence, may be illustrated by a typical encounter he had with a group of dissidents. Several persons representing the congregation of which a certain John Rogers was pastor, came to him seeking the release of their pastor. He was unjustly detained, they argued, for he had only suffered for the gospel. "I told you," Cromwell replied, "he suffered as a Railer, as a Seducer, and as a busybody . . . and a stirrer up of Sedition."[67] Impatient with the petitioners' assumption that they had liberty to do and say what they liked, that there was no limit to liberty, Cromwell thundered, "Who will hinder your preacheing of the Gospel—Yea, his [Christ's] Personal Reign, who will hinder?"[68] Then the petitioners of Rogers' congregation raised the question of liberty of conscience, to which Cromwell retorted:

> I tell you there never was such liberty of conscience, no never such liberty since the days of the Antichrist as is now—for may not men preach and pray what they will?

Significantly, he added, "And have not men their liberty of *all* opinions?"[69]

That liberty of conscience was a basic factor in the policies of the Protectorate was evident in other ways. Cromwell's friends and advisors were known advocates of liberty of conscience. Always close at hand for consultation were the principal authors of the *Apologetical Narration*, Thomas Godwin and Philip Nye, men who stated their case for liberty of conscience in that work and in others.[70] John Owen, foremost theologian of the Civil War era, was close to Cromwell. In addition to a number of tracts on liberty of conscience written after the Restoration, Owen defended the idea as he authored the *Fifteen Fundamentals of Christianity* under Cromwell's direction during the early days of the Protectorate.[71]

The Leveller John Lilburne, who was also an army officer, reports that liberty of conscience was a topic often discussed among army men. Apparently most officers saw the limit of liberty in much the same fashion as he, for he notes that General Ireton's view was an exception, that "our principal differences lie at his desire in the too strict restraining [of] liberty of conscience."[72] Lilburne adds,

> A long and tedious tug we had with Commissary General Ireton only, yea sometimes whole nights together, principally about liberty of conscience . . . and very angry and lordly in his debates many times he was.[73]

Lilburne's debates with General Ireton not only illustrate that liberty of conscience was a concern of military men, but it also shows that for them, as for Cromwell and others, the problem of the limits of liberty was central. It is noteworthy that among Cromwell and others associated with him the question of conscience had shifted from one that defended the basic claim to a question of the limits of liberty. This was not only a new aspect of the problem, but one that shows the fundamental right of conscience and its sovereignty had been accepted as a basic assumption.

In summary, concerning Cromwell and the politics of the Protectorate it is obvious that Cromwell and many of those closely associated with him embraced liberty of conscience. Cromwell himself spoke often about conscience and its liberty. His confidants, moreover, were often men associated with the religious independents, and their devotion to liberty of conscience was well known. Cromwell touched on a new aspect of liberty of conscience when he pointed out that this liberty, too, had its limits. Cromwell's devotion to and advocacy of liberty of conscience was important because he was a central political figure and for a time the most powerful man in government.

D. Conclusion

The era of the Civil War was particularly important in the history of the conflict between the ideas of toleration and liberty of conscience. The upheaval of the period brought into the open those people and factions in English society who saw merit in the claim of liberty of conscience. Earlier in the period, when Parliament called together an assembly of Divines, the range of support for liberty of conscience became evident. The Divines, either in assembly or separately in individual writings, showed how liberty of conscience was a basic idea in their thinking. Evident among them also was the relationship between liberty of conscience and sphere sovereignty, particularly in their conclusions as stated in their Confession of Faith. Their confessional statement that "God alone is Lord of conscience and has set it free from the doctrines and commandments of men" is strikingly similar to various statements on conscience made by William Perkins. While the Westminster Assembly spoke out on the question of conscience and its sovereignty, numerous members of the Leveller Movement phrased their devotion to liberty of conscience in a way that betrayed a commitment to the idea as set forth by Perkins. During the last half of the Civil War era the emergence of Oliver Cromwell as the leading political figure greatly aided the cause of conscience and its liberty. Cromwell made it clear in his statements and in the men he chose as confidants that he was devoted to liberty of conscience and that he saw it in the perspective of sphere sovereignty. Cromwell also pointed out that liberty of conscience had its limits, that it was not a license for violence. The acceptance of Perkins' view of conscience by the Westminster Assembly and Cromwellian leaders was particularly important because it represented the first occasion in which the idea gained institutional support.

In a broad perspective, the conflict between the ideas of toleration and liberty of conscience during the Civil War era must be viewed as a persistent element in the debates about the nature of English society and what it should be. The range of people and factions that could find merit in the claim of liberty of conscience has been demonstrated. A characteristic of revolutionary periods is that factions and persons may agree on one basic issue only to differ on others, and this happened often during the Civil War era. The fact remains, however, that the cause of conscience in terms of sphere sovereignty gained wide support. Toleration as an attitude toward conscience had its supporters during the Civil War era, though the shifting sands of uncertainty apparently forced them into prudent silence. The character of the Restoration, however, is evidence enough of the continuing attitude toward conscience as a phenomenon that was within the purview of governmental and church officials.

CHAPTER NOTES

1. A. F. Mitchell, *Minutes of the Sessions of the Westminster Assembly of Divines* (London, 1874); hereinafter cited as Mitchell, *Minutes*. The Ordinance calling the assembly may be found in W. W. Hetherington, *History of the Westminster Assembly of Divines* (Edinburgh, 1856), pp. 97-99; hereinafter cited as Hetherington, *History*.
2. Mitchell, *Minutes*, pp. lxxxi-lxxxvii.
3. Hetherington, *History*, p. 97.
4. *Ibid*.
5. Of the dozens of texts of the Confession, I have used that published by the United Presbyterian Church as part of its *Book of Confessions* (Philadelphia, 1966); hereinafter cited as *Confession*. The Confession begins at page 125; the statement on conscience appears on p. 141.
6. The Confession was technically adopted, but due to the fact that it occurred during the Civil War, later spokesmen for the Church of England may not regard it as ever having been part of church creeds.
7. For a good discussion of this point see C. Gordon Bolam, et al., *The English Presbyterians* (Boston, 1968), p. 73 ff.
8. *The New Schaff-Herzog Encyclopedia of Religious Knowledge* (Grand Rapids, 1950), IV, p. 167.
9. Hetherington, *History*, p. 232 ff.
10. *Ibid*.
11. *Ibid*.; see the oath that was part of the Ordinance, p. 97.
12. *Ibid*., p. 238 ff.
13. *Confession*, p. 146.
14. Mitchell, *Minutes*, p. 204.
15. *Confession*, p. 150.
16. *Ibid*., p. 144.

17. *Ibid.*
18. *Infra*, p. 178, discusses "wall of separation" and the First Amendment.
19. *Confession*, p. 150.
20. *Ibid.*, p. 144.
21. For a comment on the individual and the Reformation's idea of the priesthood of all believers see my article, "The Appeal to Conscience," *Christianity Today*, XIII (May 23, 1969), p. 5.
22. *Confession*, p. 141.
23. *Supra*, p. 4.
24. *Confession*, p. 141.
25. *Ibid.*
26. *Ibid.*
27. *Ibid.*
28. J. M. Kik, unpublished extracts made in the Dr. Williams Library, London; on deposit in the library of the Westminster Theological Seminary, Philadelphia.
29. Robert S. Paul, ed., *An Apologetical Narration* (Boston, 1963).
30. *Ibid.*, p. 2.
31. *Ibid.*
32. *Ibid.*
33. *Ibid.*
34. *Ibid.*
35. *Ibid.*, p. 3.
36. *Ibid.*
37. *Ibid.*, p. 9.
38. W. Haller and G. Davies, eds., *The Leveller Tracts 1647-1653* (New York, 1944), p. 1, n. 1.
39. Jordan, *Toleration*, III, p. 154; and William Haller, *Liberty and Reformation in the Puritan Revolution* (New York, 1955), pp. 254-287.
40. T. C. Pease, *The Leveller Movement* (Washington, 1916), p. 82.
41. William Walwyn, *The Compassionate Samaritan* (London, 1643), title page.
42. *Ibid.*, p. "A" 3.
43. *Ibid.*, p. 1.
44. *Ibid.*
45. *Ibid.*, p. 4.
46. *Ibid.*
47. *Ibid.*, p. 5.
48. *Ibid.*, p. 6.
49. *Ibid.*, p. 7.
50. *Ibid.*, pp. 10-11.
51. *Ibid.*, p. 43.
52. Henry Robinson, *Liberty of Conscience* (London, 1644), title page.

53. Richard Overton, *The Arraignment of Mr. Persecution* (London, 1645), pp. 1-3.
54. *Ibid.*, p. 4.
55. *Ibid.*
56. *Ibid.*
57. Haller, *Liberty and Reformation*, p. 256 ff., provides an introduction to Lilburne.
58. *Ibid.*, p. 238 ff.
59. Robert S. Paul, *The Lord Protector* (London, 1955), chap. XV; hereinafter cited as Paul, *Cromwell*.
60. *Ibid.*
61. Ashley, *Great Britain to 1688*, p. 357 ff.
62. Paul, *Cromwell*, p. 275 ff.
63. *Ibid.*, p. 415 ff.
64. *Ibid.*
65. *Ibid.*, p. 328.
66. *Ibid.*
67. Quoted in Paul, *Cromwell*, p. 328.
68. *Ibid.*
69. *Ibid.* (italics mine).
70. *Ibid.*, p. 324.
71. *Ibid.*, pp. 255-257.
72. *Ibid.*, p. 172, n. 4.
73. *Ibid.*

Chapter V

THE FAILURE OF LIBERTY OF CONSCIENCE IN RESTORATION ENGLAND

When Oliver Cromwell died in September, 1658, he was succeeded by his son Richard, but Richard was neither the soldier nor the "saint" that his father had been. He was not able to control the army, it becoming factious as did Republican partisans generally. By summer of 1959 army men were openly divided, one group being led by General Monck. Monck was on duty in Scotland, and having declared his support for civil rather than military government, marched on London. Other military leaders opposed him, but they found little support among the citizenry. Monck arrived in London, restored parliamentary members that had been excluded in 1648, and persuaded them to make way for a newly elected Commons. Finally Monck negotiated for the return of Charles II, outmaneuvering parliamentary attempts to impose specific terms upon the king. Charles arrived in London in May, 1660, welcomed by delirious crowds.[1]

The arrival of Charles signaled the end of the Civil War, the beginning of the Restoration era, and, more significantly, the end of the experimentation in England with liberty of conscience as an option to the tradition of mere toleration. How it happened that liberty of conscience did not endure as a matter of policy in England is something requiring explanation. Noteworthy also is the fact that the failure of liberty of conscience as a policy option brought about renewed persecution and, finally, the Toleration Act of 1689. In a broader perspective, Restoration policy concerning the rights of conscience assured a divergence in attitude between England and her American colonies on the question of liberty of conscience. The extent and meaning of this divergence will be evident in subsequent chapters.

The fate of liberty of conscience during the Restoration era depended upon the character of the settlement that brought Charles II back to England. For a decade after his father's death, Charles plotted ways to regain his throne, but he had no money and few friends. There was irony in the fact that all his plotting failed, only to be supplanted by an invitation to return. That he was invited to return, however, colored the nature of the subsequent settlement. As a condition of his return Charles agreed to publish a declaration from Breda in Holland stating that he would leave to a future parliament many important decisions of policy and that he would grant liberty to tender consciences. Charles issued his declaration and it was approved by the "Convention" Parliament in April of 1660.[2]

That provision was made in the declaration for the problem of tender consciences indicates that government representatives, as well as Charles, recognized the critical nature of this issue in the public mind. The fate of liberty of conscience must be assessed in the context of the main problems that confronted the settlement of a government. Six problems were of major proportion: the future of the army, of religion, and of finance, the settlement of landed property, and return to monarchical government, and the punishment of offenders against the Stuart kings.[3] As for the military, it would have been dangerous to retain a large standing army that had been so deeply involved in the Cromwellian Republic. Apart from a unit or two that were retained, later to be known as the Coldstream Guards, the army was paid off and disbanded. Any settlement of the property question was bound to create enemies. Titles to much property had been disturbed by the Civil War, some parcels had been sequestered, while others had been conveyed under Republican statutes. The settlement restored Crown lands and church property. Recent studies indicate no revolutionary change in property ownership resulted from the Civil War. The question of punishment of anti-royalists was covered by a general pardon excepting a few persons such as General Harrison and Henry Vane, who were directly involved in the execution of King Charles I. As for the constitution, statutes assented to by Charles I, even under pressure, retained their validity. In general, the *status quo* of 1641 was reinstated. Finance was a complex issue. The main point was, however, that Charles II was voted a revenue of 1.2 million pounds, an amount that in time allowed him to assume great independence of Parliament.[4]

In the resolution of these problems the normative principle was "restoration," not revolution. This implied an end to constitutional experimentation. The settlement sought to bridge the gap between the earlier monarchy and that of Charles II.

Of the major problems that confronted the settlement of government, none was more important for the question of liberty of conscience than the religious question. This issue cannot, of course, be totally separated from the others already mentioned, but it may be separated for more detailed examination.

From the point of view of advocates of liberty of conscience the religious climate of the Restoration era consisted of two moods: hope and despair. During the first months it appeared that liberty of conscience would be part of the religious settlement. Charles himself declared from Breda "a liberty to tender consciences." This declaration was approved by the "Convention" Parliament, the body negotiating the return of Charles. Many London ministers viewed this declaration as a signal that they, as Presbyterian ministers, would be included in a comprehensive church settlement. Some ministers even discussed the matter with Charles before he left Breda. Soon after he arrived in London a number of ministers again talked over the church question with him, distinguishing themselves from others who were disturbers of the peace.[5]

In subsequent meetings the ministers pointed out specific evils that they found in the Church of England as it existed before 1640 and they offered remedies. Many of these, of course, had to do with practices such as garb to be worn and elements of liturgy. Charles declared his intention of calling an assembly of divines to settle the questions before him. After numerous exchanges with dissenting ministers, and with bishops as well, he decided that all parties were too contentious to come to any resolution. In place of an assembly he decided to make his own statement on the religious question, intending it to serve until the time was appropriate for an assembly. In October, therefore, he issued a statement on religious policy.[6] Among many other items it called for liberty of conscience, as he reminded his subjects that this was the stand he had taken in the Breda declaration.

Soon after Charles's declaration on the religious question the London ministers wrote the king and thanked him for his understanding of their interests. The mood of optimism continued among them, as was evident in their reply. As for liberty of conscience, they wrote,

> The liberty of our consciences, and the free exercise of our ministry in the work of our great Lord and Master, for the conversion of souls, ought to be, and are, more dear to us than all the profits and preferments of this world; and therefore your majesty's tenderness, manifest in these so high concernments, doth wonderfully affect us, and raise up our hearts to a high pitch of gratitude.[7]

As the new year began, a fanatical group of Fifth Monarchists staged a four-day uprising in London, precipitating a royal circumscription of private meetings. Numerous sects rushed letters to the king explaining that they as Quakers, Anabaptists, and Independents had nothing to do with the radical sectarians. Meanwhile a number of London Presbyterians mounted a concerted effort toward electing their representatives to the House in the forthcoming elections. Royalists in the government were alarmed, their reaction being a measure of their sensitivity, their apprehension. Neither the actions of fanatics nor the election designs of London Presbyterians suggest that the degree of optimism, so evident during the previous year, was still entertained by dissenters.

A week after the London elections, however, a warrant was issued for the long promised assembly of divines. It called for a meeting in Savoy Palace and named an equal number of divines from each of the two main divisions within the religious community—Anglicans and Dissenters.[8] The warrant was cordial and bolstered the hopes of the dissenting community. The key to the success of this conference, however, rested not on what might be determined by it, but rather in how or by whom it might be approved. The disputants entered debate with much energy, as the lengthy assembly documents attest, but it soon became evident that recrimination was all that could be expected from the conference.

Although the Savoy conference was charged with revising the Book of Common Prayer, the Convocation was busy with its own revision even before the Savoy conference ended. It had been evident from the moment Charles returned that an episcopal government would prevail, but that in itself was not necessarily a bar to many Presbyterians. By the time the Savoy conference ended, it was clear that the form of episcopal government would be no different from that which had existed in 1640. The work of Convocation, therefore, in revising Common Prayer went a long way toward creating a uniformity that would be unacceptable to Presbyterians.[9]

Cause for optimism, cause for hope that dissenting parties could or would be included in the religious settlement, vanished by the summer of 1661. The problem of comprehension within the Church now became a question of how dissenters would be treated outside of the Church. The elections of 1661 created a Parliament that was hostile to Puritans of all types, for it was a Parliament of Anglican and royalist interests.[10]

The extent of royalist sentiment in the Parliament of 1661, or Cavalier Parliament, was evident in the measures it passed. The king was given supreme control over all the armed forces of land and sea; he was given extraordinary power in a new treason law. Aided by a new official, the Surveyor of Imprimery, he now had extensive power over authors and printers, a measure aimed at limiting the ability of citizens to petition him. Parliament also passed the Corporation Act, which was designed to limit the membership in corporations to Anglicans and loyal royalists.[11]

These measures were followed by the Act of Uniformity.[12] It provided that everyone who held any ecclesiastical office prior to St. Bartholomew's Day, 1662, had to, on that day, read the morning and evening prayers, and then in public before the congregation declare his assent to everything contained in and prescribed by the Book of Common Prayer. In addition, the Solemn League and

Covenant had to be renounced. Moreover, after that day only those who had received episcopal ordination in the Church of England could officiate in it. The Act covered tutors and schoolmasters as well as parish ministers. Innumerable possible offenses were mentioned in the Act, breaches being covered by explicit penalties.

Hope of liberty of conscience was utterly and brutally extinguished in the provisions of the Act of Uniformity; at least it was for the dissenting ministers. As St. Bartholomew's Day approached in 1662, thousands of ministers had to make a decision whether they would abide by the provisions of the Act. Some two thousand could not. They chose to be cut off from the Church of England rather than submit to its provisions. This event is known to history as the Great Ejection. Some ejected ministers found refuge in the homes of wealthy friends; others turned to different vocations to support themselves and their families; still others migrated.[13]

Though the Corporation Act struck at Puritans in business, while the Act of Uniformity disabled dissenting ministers, little had been done to curtail the religious privileges of the average citizen, until the Conventicle Act of 1664.[14] This Act struck at the mass of dissenting brethren in the churches. Its main feature provided penalties for anyone caught at a religious meeting not conducted according to the liturgy of the Church of England, provided he was at least sixteen years of age. The penalties consisted of fines for the first two offenses, thereafter, seven years in certain American colonies. A year later, in 1665, still another measure was passed to harass dissenters, it being the Five Mile Act, which prevented ministers and teachers from approaching within five miles of any place where they had formerly been employed.[15]

It is important to note that these measures against dissenters were passed and enforced by Parliament. Civil officers, and on occasion the militia, were used to enforce them. During the early years of the Restoration, enforcement was pursued with vigor; in the 1670's and 1680's they were enforced fitfully, according to the whims of expedient government officials. Churchmen, of course, had a stake in the program of harassment of dissenters, but once the latter had been effectively excluded from the Church, Church leaders were free of the disruptive element.

As for Charles's role in the suppression of dissenters, historians differ. One view is expressed in the following estimate of him:

> The King himself was not a fanatic. A dark man with a large nose, over six feet tall, he had been a good-looking boy, but had grown into a rather ugly, if strangely attractive, man. He was a dilettante, inclined to be lazy but capable of bursts of energy. Good-looking women and entertaining rogues gave him pleasure, but scarcely influenced his policies. If he had any principles, they were to maintain his throne and his dynasty intact.[16]

Another historian states, "For these severities, little, if any, blame can be attached to Charles himself."[17] Charles's repeated statement that he believed in liberty of conscience may, of course, be viewed cynically, his statements being explained as a matter of expedient policy. A case might be made, however, for the claim that Charles was forced to acquiesce in the matter of liberty and toleration if he wished to maintain any support in Parliament. Charles's attitude toward liberty of conscience will be examined more fully in the subsequent discussion of the growth of liberty of conscience in the American Colonies.

The character of the Restoration religious settlement was thus largely the work of the Cavalier Parliament. Before it came to power in the summer of 1661, advocates of liberty of conscience had reason to believe that they would enjoy this liberty as a right mandated by the Restoration government. Their belief was based upon the fact that the "Convention" Parliament was conciliatory, and upon the declarations of the king himself. This hope was short-lived, for soon after it convened, the Cavalier Parliament enacted numerous severe measures. These measures not only precluded the recognition of the rights of conscience, they called for a vigorous campaign of repression of dissent. While some seats of this Parliament were changed through by-elections, it remained intact and in power for nineteen years. The Cavalier Parliament thus dominated the character of the religious climate in England for the greater part of the Restoration era.

THE FAILURE IN RESTORATION ENGLAND

The various measures of Parliament effectively excluded dissenters from the Church of England, from corporations, and other positions of privilege. These measures did not, however, completely silence the advocacy of liberty of conscience. Throughout the Restoration era in England there were always people advocating and defending the need for liberty of conscience.

As the Restoration began, for example, John Milton continued his defense of liberty, something he had done early in the Civil War. In 1659 he wrote a tract on the power of government in ecclesiastical affairs in which he argued vigorously for the cause of sphere sovereignty. He called upon the whole history of state churches as evidence of the cause of the problems that plagued England. He stressed the evil of enslavement of the individual soul by clergy aligned with the power of the state. Heresy was one of the keys in the chain that bound men's consciences. Milton could find no clear meaning for this word *heresy* in the Greek language from which it came; to him it meant only that men differed in opinions. Milton placed conscience in the center of his argument against heresy:

> Seeing ... that no man, no synod, no session of men, though called the Church, can judge definitively the sense of scripture to another man's conscience, which is well known to be a general maxim of the Protestant religion, it follows plainly, that he who holds in religion that belief or those opinions which to his conscience and utmost understanding appear with most evidence or probability in the scripture, though to others seem erroneous, can no more be justly censured, for a heretic than his censures; who do but the same thing themselves while they censure him for so doing.[18]

More positively, he wrote that Protestants "granted rule of every man's conscience to himself," that is, conscience was at liberty in relation to all other men.[19]

Another example of the defense of liberty of conscience in the early days of the Restoration was the noted political philosopher, James Harrington. Harrington's most famous work, *Oceana*, had been published in 1656 and was dedicated to Oliver Cromwell.[20] This work outlined in detail many items of government that were to find embodiment in the American system of government, such as rotation of offices, secret ballots, and government based upon a written instrument. *Oceana* defended religious liberty based upon liberty of conscience, but with the passing of Cromwell in 1658 and the changing political climate of 1659, Harrington wrote numerous additional tracts on facets of government all of which gave a prominent role to liberty of conscience. Harrington's persistence as a republican and defender of liberty of conscience led to his imprisonment in 1661.

He defined liberty of conscience as that condition of society in which "a man according to the dictates of his own conscience may have the free exercise of his religion" without regard to his place or station in relation to government.[21] He linked liberty of conscience to civil liberty, "without liberty of conscience, civil liberty cannot be perfect; and without civil liberty, liberty of conscience cannot be perfect."[22] A good government is one that will create a climate in which its citizens are able "to make use of their liberty of conscience."[23] Harrington's works, like Milton's, were read and quoted much in the years of the Restoration and after.

Another eloquent and influential defender of liberty of conscience during the Restoration was John Owen. During the Civil War, Owen had been friend and confidant of Cromwell, a leading spokesman for the so-called independents, and a leader in the Oxford community. The effect of the Restoration on Owen and his work is interesting because it is representative of how a limited number of dissenting ministers handled themselves during the period, a number who were so well known and so close to the center of power that they received special, though not always kind, treatment.

While at Oxford it had been Owen's habit to preach often in the village of Stadham, the place of his birth, and as the Restoration began he went there, hoping to be left to his scholarly work. With the Act of Uniformity and other measures it became necessary for him to give up preaching to the small congregation in Stadham. Owen sought an interview with Sir Edward Hyde, the lord chancellor, in the hope of easing the severity of the policies against dissenters.

Hyde insisted that Owen refrain from preaching, but at the same time he asked Owen to write against Roman Catholicism. Hyde's motives seemed obvious. He could use the considerable talent of Owen in a most important area and therein hope to divert his attention from the dissenting cause.[24]

Owen continued to preach in small secret gatherings, and in time he began to write the treatise suggested by Sir Edward Hyde. Owen's target was a work written by the Franciscan John Vincent Cane on the subject of the differences between Catholics and Protestants. The thrust of Cane's message was that peace could come among Christians only at such time as they all joined the Church of Rome, though the message was more subtly stated. Owen described the author as having the voice of Jacob and the hands of Esau. Owen's critique elicited a rejoinder and that in turn was answered by Owen.[25]

Owen's refutation of the Franciscan's works received wide attention. Sir Edward Hyde in an interview with Owen offered the opinion that Owen had done more for the cause of Protestantism than any other man in England, but Hyde could not understand how such a talented man could be misled by the notion of independency.[26] Hyde suggested that Owen could hold a high office in the Church if he gave up his old opinions about church government. Owen argued that the congregation was the basic unit described in the New Testament and the pattern followed by the early church, but he was not able to gain support for this view from the lord chancellor.

Soon after these exchanges with Hyde, probably in early 1664, John Owen was invited to serve as pastor in John Cotton's old pulpit in Boston, New England. What response Owen gave to this invitation is not entirely clear except that he did not go to New England. One writer has it that he desired to go, but was stopped by an order of the court.[27] Another writer states that he was unwilling to leave the cause of dissenters at home, resolving to wait for happier days.[28]

Owen's activities during the next three years suggest that had he gone to New England, his auditors there would have been displeased with his view of the dissenting cause. Upon hearing how the New

Englanders treated dissenters, Owen joined other leading dissenters in England and wrote them a letter of rebuke. It requested the following:

> That you will trust God with his truth and ways, so far as to suspend all rigorous proceedings in corporeal restraints or punishments on persons that dissent from you, and practice principles of their dissent without danger or disturbance to the civil peace of the place.[29]

This was written at the time that Owen was writing a number of tracts on the subject of liberty, items that would have been distasteful to New Englanders. One tract was on the "Grounds and Reasons on which the Protestant Dissenters Desire their Liberty." Another was a "Humble Plea for Liberty of Conscience."[30]

Meanwhile the Great Plague, followed in 1666 by the great London fire, diverted the attention of the government and churchmen; thus the lot of dissenters was eased. The fall of Sir Edward Hyde's government the following year further complicated the religious climate. Some church leaders, such as Bishop Wilkins of Chester, saw this as an occasion to enlarge toleration and thus quiet the strife that had engulfed society for most of the decade. Though this plan was endorsed by prominent churchmen, such as Tillotson and Stillingfleet, it was violently opposed by others. Supporters of suppression were forced to defend their position, and their view appeared in a tract by Samuel Parker.

The dispute among Anglican churchmen is interesting because it shows support among them for the cause of dissent. More important, however, is the work written by Parker, for it stated clearly the rationale with which dissenters such as Owen had to contend. Parker's title page summed up very adequately what could be found in the text. The short-title was "Discourse of Ecclesiastical Polity, and of the Power of the Magistrate in Matters of Religion."[31] The longer title included the following, "the authority of the civil magistrate over the consciences of subjects in matters of external religion is asserted, the mischief and inconveniences of toleration are represented, and all pretences pleaded in favor of liberty of conscience are fully answered."[32]

John Owen replied in his *Truth and Innocence Vindicated.* Like Parker's work, Owen's full title stated the thrust of his purpose: A Survey of a Discourse Concerning Ecclesiastical Polity, and the Authority of the Civil Magistrate Over the Consciences of Subjects in Matters of Religion.[33] This is Owen's most comprehensive work on liberty of conscience, it covering two hundred pages in fine print. It states clearly and fully the case for liberty of conscience in terms of sphere sovereignty, and thus it marks Owen as a leading apologist.

Since the document is a line by line refutation of Parker's Discourse, it will suffice to indicate only briefly some of the main points made by Owen. He began the essay by pointing out the basic problem that confronts anyone who decides to enter a debate about liberty of conscience, namely, that if one really believes that liberty of conscience is "the direct will and command of God, there is no point to the debate.[34] If the matter is to be debated at all, therefore, it can proceed only upon a supposition. In Owen's words, "Among the many disadvantages which those who plead in any sense for liberty of conscience are exposed unto, is not the least that . . . they are enforced to admit a supposition."[35] This was an important point, for it opened the door to a more adequate distinction between the question of the right of liberty of conscience and the question of the limits of liberty.

Owen immediately reinforced his contention that professors of liberty of conscience really had nothing to debate by observing that "men, therefore, in such discourses, speak not to the nature of the things themselves, but to the apprehensions of them" by their opponents.[36] In other words, in the essay he was beginning, he was not questioning the existence of liberty of conscience, only the manner in which Parker understood it. Making this distinction, Owen's argument was much more forceful.

Having stated the grounds on which he intended to stand as he examined Parker's treatise, Owen went on to review Parker's introduction. It made bold and raucous claims, said Owen, claims which the text of the treatise did not support nor prove. As for liberty of conscience, Parker said that he demonstrated the "inconsistence of liberty of conscience with the first and fundamental laws of government."[37] Said Owen of this,

> I am content that he please himself with his own apprehensions, like him who admired at the marvelous feats performed in an empty theatre . . . there is scarce in his whole discourse any one argument offered that hath the least seeming cogency towards such an end.[38]

Further, said Owen, "whether you take 'liberty of conscience' for liberty of judgment, which himself confesseth uncontrolable, or liberty of practice" which he opposes, you will not even find his conclusion, much less his premise.[39]

Turning from Parker's form of argument, Owen examined his contention that men could not live peacefully if they enjoyed "the liberty of their consciences." That they could was demonstrated in several states on the Continent, in Owen's view. Finally he mentioned Parker's position that it was erroneous to believe that " 'liberty of conscience would conduce much to the improvement of trade in the nation.' "[40] Many people who were deeply involved in the econnomic affairs of the nation supported the contention that liberty of conscience was helpful to trade, said Owen, and he was willing to take their word for it rather than that of Parker.

In short, Owen's review of Parker's introduction demonstrates Owen's belief that Parker did not approach the central issue in the problem, that is, whether liberty of conscience was a right; moreover, the objections that Parker did in fact raise were on shaky ground. Owen's review also indicates his own view of liberty of conscience and something of the tenacity with which he held it.

The main body of Owen's treatise reflects other aspects of his view of liberty of conscience. As for the source of authority for conscience, "The power of God over the consciences of men I suppose is acknowledged by all who own any such thing as conscience, or believe there is a God over all."[41] More specifically, there is "government of the consciences of men . . . and that in subjection to and dependence on Christ alone." Conscience, therefore,

> . . . is the practical judgment that men make of themselves and

of their actions, or what they are to do and what they are not to do, what they have done or what they have omitted, with reference unto the judgment of God, at present declared in their own hearts and his word, and to be fully executed at the last day....[42]

As Owen stressed the positive aspect of the meaning of liberty of conscience, he also stated its relationship to the nature and duties of government. The business of government and its magistrates was distinct from other aspects of human experience, he often repeated in this treatise. Typically he spoke of magistrates who "kept themselves to their proper sphere" as princes who thereby made themselves "dear to mankind."[43] The end of government was "the preservation of public peace and tranquillity in the world." God "who is the fountain and original of all power hath both assigned its government's proper end, and fully suited it to the attainment thereof." The problems that plagued English society did not stem from anything else than the clamor of greedy men, said Owen. If they could be silent, "we should quickly hear the harmonious consenting voice of human nature itself declaring the just proportion that is between the grant of power and its end."[44]

These observations on the scope and purpose of government were made in an attempt to refute Parker's claim concerning the magistrate that " 'religion is subject of his dominion, as well as all other affairs of state.' " They show that Owen believed in the integrity of the individual and in the liberty of his conscience, that this liberty was part of a general ordering of creation that included the political state. The grant of power to the state was for a specific end, that is, preserving the peace and tranquillity of society. The state had no authority over conscience, and it had no authority over the church. The latter point Owen often made in this essay.

Parker's claim that government had authority over religion led to serious distortions in the affairs of religion, said Owen. Parker's scheme led to the establishment of the magistrate on an equal footing with the Lord and of the church. In Owen's words,

> The authority ascribed to the civil magistrate being as hath been expressed, it will be very hard for any one to distinguish between

it and the sovereignty that the Lord Christ himself hath in and over the church; yea, if there be any advantage on either side, or a comparative preeminence, it will be found to be cast upon that of the magistrate.[45]

For Owen, the matter of worship, the nature of gathered groups of believers, is a matter that is distinct from the affairs of the state, a matter under the direct authority of Christ.

Owen's *Truth and Innocence Vindicated* was a smashing success. It drew from Parker a reply as vindictive as any piece written in that age of venomous rhetoric. Owen was "the great bell-wether of disturbance and sedition," a person "who would have vied with Mahomet himself both for boldness and imposture," and "a viper so swollen with venom that it must either burst or spit its poison." Parker suggested that his true countrymen could do no better service to it "than by beating down the interest and reputation of such sons of Belial."[46]

A measure of Owen's success and a clue to how a dissenter of his stature was treated during the Restoration may also be found in the effect that his exchanges with Parker had on other writers. A friend of Milton's, Andrew Marvell, reviewed Parker's work in his *Rehearsal Transposed.* Said Marvell of Parker,

> If he chance but to sneeze, he prays that the foundations of the earth be not shaken. Ever since he crept up to be but the weathercock of a steeple, he trembles and cracks at every puff of wind that blows about him, as if the Church of England were falling.[47]

One student of Marvell reports that even the royal court joined the laughter generated by Marvell's witty critique of Parker and his writings.

Even after his essay on the power of magistrates Owen continued to enjoy interviews with the king, always pressing the cause of dissenters. Through the efforts of Sir John Trevor, a principal secretary of state, Owen was invited to meet with the king and his brother, the duke of York, at Turnbridge Wells.[48] Liberty for dissenters was extensively discussed, and the king expressed his wish that they could be relieved of their strictures. Subsequent to this meeting Owen met with the king often in London, and on occasion the king gave Owen money to help relieve the sufferings of poor dissenters.⁴⁹ These meetings with the king occurred during the months prior to the Declaration of Indulgence of 1672, though it is not clear that Owen had any direct influence on the policy. Owen's efforts did not go unnoticed among his enemies. Said one,

> Witness his fishing out the king's counsels, and inquiring whether things went well to his great Diana, liberty of conscience? how his majesty stood affected to it? whether he would connive at it and the execution of the laws against it? who were or could be made his friends at court? what bills were like to be put to Parliament?⁵⁰

Owen lived until 1683, dying in August on St. Bartholomew's Day, the anniversary of the ejection of so many of his dissenting brethren. Though he continued his public career until his last days, he spent much of his time writing numerous tracts and treatises. Some of these were published after his death, and among them were several on liberty of conscience. Owen thus continued his defense of liberty of conscience to the end of his life.

The impact of the work of men like Owen on behalf of liberty of conscience during the Restoration is difficult to measure with precision. Owen's dispute with Parker, his other tracts, and his frequent discussions with King Charles undoubtedly left their mark. At the same time, it was obvious that the character of the religious settlement and the enforcement of it depended upon the whims of the Cavalier Parliament and the relationship between it and the Crown.

While it is noteworthy that defenders of liberty of conscience continued to speak and write despite the repressive climate of the Restoration, the value of their work rests also in the fact that it contributed to the solution of the problem of dissent in the Glorious Revolution. Not that the claim of liberty of conscience triumphed in the Revolution; rather, it reinforced the movement in favor of a more liberal toleration of dissent.

The Toleration Act of 1689 embodied the provisions Parliament was willing to extend to dissenters.⁵¹ It was not generous, but it did give legal standing to a variety of dissenters. The old persecuting acts were not removed by it; they were merely suspended in certain cases. Non-conforming parties could worship in separate places provided they secured a license for it and left the doors open when meeting. The document itself ran to some five thousand words, an indication of the spirit in which it was written, an indication of the assumption that the limits of toleration must necessarily be defined in great detail.

This measure helped to stabilize the political and religious climate during the years following the Restoration era, but as one student of the problem has said, it also helped to relegate dissenters to the backwaters of English society.[52] The measure removed none of the disadvantages that accrued to the non-members of the Church of England; as under the Restoration, they were almost entirely excluded from positions of responsibility and trust, and their sons still could not attend the universities. They might be able to worship God as they pleased, but it was difficult to serve the king.

In terms of the contest between liberty of conscience and toleration in England, the Toleration Act ended the dispute. Liberty of conscience as a step-child of the Reformation came to life in England during the Age of Elizabeth under the leadership of the Cambridge Puritan Brotherhood. It grew under their care and feeding and became increasingly a staple in the storehouse of ideas preached during the first half of the seventeenth century. As the Civil War began, the claim for liberty of conscience, nourished so long by so many, came to be the center of the debate on church and state. It even became a basic prop in the state governed by Oliver Cromwell. With the coming of the Restoration the fate of liberty of conscience was not at once clear, for Charles himself was one of its advocates. Amidst the rapid rise of Restoration sentiment and under the hand of the Cavalier Parliament a religious settlement emerged that was hostile to the claim of liberty of conscience. A few eloquent, and surely courageous, souls continued to press for liberty of conscience despite the hostile climate of the Restoration era.

As for toleration, it had always been the policy of English governments, its roots being somewhere in the deep past. Its significance in England dates from the beginning of the Age of Elizabeth, for she was the one who held out the prospect of a true reformation of the English Church. Queen Elizabeth formulated a policy of toleration that went beyond mere personal whim, and therein set the pattern for her successors. She did not, however, elevate her policy to the level of formal statement or statute. Subsequently the degree of toleration could vary with the needs and personal wishes of the monarch or his government, and it did. James I talked of toleration and even liberty, but behaved in a vacillating way. Charles I, led by the designs of Bishop Laud, tolerated little in the way of dissent. The harshness of his stance was a contributing factor in the cause of the Civil War. Of course, there were advocates of toleration in the Civil War, but in this era they had to compete with the open claim of liberty of conscience. Since the return of the monarchy was a conscious attempt to restore the old order, toleration was prominent in the settlement, notwithstanding the efforts of Charles himself. The attitude toward dissent on the part of the government during the Restoration was as harsh as it had been at any time in a century.

Theoretically, it could be argued, there was still a chance that liberty of conscience could supplant mere toleration as the Glorious Revolution began in 1688. In fact, that was not possible, for the case for liberty of conscience had been presented during the Civil War, and when it was rejected in the first months of the Restoration, it found new life in the colonies of America. A few advocates of it remained; fewer still were willing to press the claim of liberty of conscience as a right in the unhospitable climate of the Restoration. Thus, as the Revolution came in 1688, the only hope for the problem of dissent in England rested in a formal recognition of a moderate policy of toleration, and that happened in the Toleration Act of 1689. This measure regulated the problem of dissent in England until the era of reform in the 1830's. Advocates of liberty of conscience, therefore, had to look elsewhere for a climate congenial to their argument.

CHAPTER NOTES

1. Maurice Ashley, *Great Britain to 1688* (Ann Arbor, 1961). I have used this essay as a guide to affairs in England during the Restoration. Many other works cited in the notes to this chapter cover the same events and may be compared with Ashley's views. Hereinafter it will be cited as

Ashley, *Britain*. The material referred to in this note may be found on p. 368 ff.
2. *Ibid.*
3. *Ibid.*
4. *Ibid.*
5. The text of the declaration may be found in George Gould, *Documents Relating to the Settlement of the Church of England by the Act of Uniformity of 1662* (London, 1862), pp. 1-3. The pagination in this volume is confusing because the introductory essay on Puritanism, written by Peter Bayne, is also numbered in Arabic.
6. *Ibid.*, p. 104 ff.
7. *Ibid.*, p. 101 ff.
8. *Ibid.*, p. 107 ff.
9. Ashley, *Britain*, p. 368 ff.
10. *Ibid.*
11. *Ibid.*
12. *Ibid.*; for text see Gould, *Documents*, p. 386 ff.
13. A. G. Matthews, *Calamy Revised* (Oxford, 1934). The introduction to this essay gives a full account of the Ejection. It is a valuable tool for the study of the effect of the Settlement upon dissenters, being a modern study of a contemporary review of the problem.
14. Ashley, *Britain*, p. 368 ff.
15. *Ibid.*, and for text see Gould, *Documents*, p. 488 ff.
16. Ashley, *Britain*, pp. 373-374.
17. G. R. Cragg, *From Puritanism to the Age of Reason* (Cambridge, 1966), p. 221.
18. John Milton, *Treatise of Civil Power, Works* (London, 1659), p. 311.
19. *Ibid.*
20. James Harrington, *The Commonwealth of Oceana* (London, 1656).
21. James Harrington, *A System of Politics* (London, 1700), pp. 505-506.
22. James Harrington, *Valerius and Publicola* (London, 1659), p. 489.
23. James Harrington, *Humble Petition, Works* (London, 1659), p. 544.
24. To my knowledge there has not been a modern study of John Owen, though the works of numerous scholars point to the fact that he was an important figure in seventh-century English life. His writings were published as *The Works of John Owen* (Edinburgh, 1850-1853), ed., Wm. H. Goold, and reprinted by the Banner of Truth Trust, London, beginning in 1965. Various aspects of his career cited in the text are taken from the 122-page introduction to his works, hereinafter cited as Owen, *Works*. For Owen's relationship to Hyde see p. lxviii ff. (vol. 1).
25. *Ibid.*, p. lxxix ff.
26. *Ibid.*
27. *Ibid.*

THE FAILURE IN RESTORATION ENGLAND 127

28. *Ibid.*
29. *Ibid.*, p. lxxxvii.
30. *Ibid.* These items are collected in vol. XIII, beginning on p. 576.
31. *Ibid.*, XIII, p. 343. Here begins Owen's tract against Parker, including a description of Parker's work.
32. *Ibid.*
33. *Ibid.*
34. *Ibid.*, p. 345.
35. *Ibid.*
36. *Ibid.*
37. *Ibid.*, p. 366.
38. *Ibid.*
39. *Ibid.*
40. *Ibid.*, p. 367.
41. *Ibid.*, p. 440.
42. *Ibid*
43. *Ibid.*, p. 498.
44. *Ibid.*, p. 492.
45. *Ibid.*, p. 377.
46. *Ibid.*, I, p. lxxxix.
47. *Ibid.*
48. *Ibid.*, p. xci.
49. *Ibid.*
50. *Ibid.*, xcii.
51. G. R. Cragg, *Puritanism in the Period of the Great Persecution* (Cambridge, 1957), p. 248 ff.; for the text of the Act, see Gould, *Documents*, p. 507 ff.
52. *Ibid.*, p. 251.

Chapter VI

THE ACCEPTANCE OF LIBERTY OF CONSCIENCE IN AMERICA: 1630-1770

The conflict between the ideas of toleration and liberty of conscience in Old England, a conflict that was resolved in the Toleration Act of 1689, spilled over into the English colonies in America, but with a different result. In America the claim of liberty of conscience became an important element in thought and practice among the earliest settlers, the idea gaining support until it was set forth as a fundamental principle in the constitutional fabric of the American Revolution. In short, liberty of conscience triumphed in America, while it failed in England.

In a broad perspective, the most important phase in the history of liberty of conscience in America encompasses the two decades (1770-1790) covering the American Revolution, for during this period the new states all provided for liberty of conscience in their constitutions, the same protection appearing in the new federal constitution. These events all appear as a decisive, and even dramatic, move to insure a guarantee of liberty of conscience in the new nation. They will thus be examined together in the following chapter.

In turning to an examination of the evidence of liberty of conscience during the period 1630-1770, it is clear that interest in conscience and its liberty appeared early and spread throughout most of the colonies by the end of the seventeenth century, Massachusetts Bay Colony being the major exception. It is also clear that as the seventeenth century came to a close, liberty of conscience, together with its parallel concept of sphere sovereignty, was a part of an emerging American political ideology. From the perspective of the triumph of liberty of conscience at the time of the Revolution, it will be useful to view the early arrival and spread of liberty of conscience as one phase of the development of the idea in America, thereafter examining the relationship of it to the emerging political ideology. The evidence also lends itself to this distinction, for during the period 1630-1689 the outstanding expressions of devotion to the cause of conscience and its liberty appeared in local laws and, more importantly, in charters. Many individuals, of course, spoke for the cause, too. By the end of the century, however, expressions concerning conscience and sovereignty were made in the context of political issues, such as the question of state authority over churches and over individuals.

The discussion of liberty of conscience in pre-Revolutionary America will thus be divided into two phases. First, the period 1630-1689 will be examined with special attention given to individual and institutional expressions of the idea. Following this, the period 1689-1770 will be surveyed, attention being given to the relationship between liberty of conscience and the emerging political ideology.

A. *Liberty of Conscience in the American Colonies: 1630-1689*

An earlier chapter outlined the fate of liberty of conscience in the Massachusetts Bay Colony.[1] Massachusetts Bay leaders resisted and denied the claim of liberty of conscience, relying on Amesian orthodoxy for their arguments. These leaders had been challenged by Roger Williams and, later, Anne Hutchinson, both of whom claimed that conscience was at liberty in relation to other men and institutions.

While the Massachusetts Bay position on liberty of consience was reviewed in some detail, little was said about the views of others outside of that colony. In fact, liberty of conscience spread rapidly throughout the other colonies during the years that it was being resisted in Massachusetts Bay. Winthrop himself was aware of this and recorded his impression in his Journal for December, 1638. He wrote:

> At Providence, also, the devil was not idle. For whereas, at their first coming thither, Mr. Williams and the rest did make an order, that no man should be molested for his conscience . . . (concern-

ing the censure of a person for his attitude toward the role of women in the churches). In conclusion, when they would have censured Verin, Arnold told them, that it was against their own order, for Verin did that which he did out of conscience; and their order was, that no man should be censured for his conscience.²

Later he wrote, "Many books [are] coming out of England, some in defense of anabaptism and other errors, and for liberty of conscience as shelter for their toleration."³ In 1648 Winthrop reported on the visit of a pastor, Mr. Haryson, from Virginia, who told him that his congregation had grown to over one hundred members and that Governor Berkeley was harassing them. Haryson inquired whether Winthrop thought they should leave Virginia. He told Winthrop that they could go to the Bahama Islands where one, William Sayle, planned a colony, having been granted a charter by Parliament. Winthrop advised him not to go and commented on the provisions of the charter for the Bahamian colony:

> The first article was for liberty of conscience, wherein they provided, that the civil magistrate should not have cognizance of any matter which concerned religion, but every man might enjoy his own opinion or religion, without control or question, (nor was there any word of maintaining or professing any religion or worship of God at all). . . .⁴

Winthrop undoubtedly thought that the devil was at work in the islands as well as in Providence. Closer to home, during the Dr. Child's affair, Winthrop noted that in the search of the possessions of Child's associates, Bay agents found a petition addressed to Parliament which pleaded the need for "liberty of conscience, etc. . . ." in the Bay colony.⁵

There were other claims for liberty of conscience in the colonies in addition to those Winthrop commented on. The emergence of liberty of conscience noted by him in Providence in 1638 was confirmed in a plantation agreement written in the summer of 1640. It said, "We agree, as formerly hath been the liberties of the town, so still, to hold forth liberty of conscience."⁶ The document was signed by thirty-nine people. Rufus Jones, noted Quaker historian, rehearsed a dispute between the Dutch governor of New York and the townspeople of Flushing, Long Island, in his study of Quakers in the American colonies. He indicates that liberty of conscience was central in the dispute:

> The inhabitants of Flushing were profoundly stirred by this invasion of their liberties. They gathered in a public meeting, expressed their disapproval of the acts of persecution, and drew up a remonstrance which was signed by thirty-one men and sent to the Governor. . . . The remonstrance declared that the patent, or charter, of their town "grants liberty of conscience without modification," and that the signers intended to stand by their precious rights. . . .[7]

The question of the rights of conscience was basic in the early settlement of Maryland, also. The Act Concerning Religion of 1649 is often referred to by students of religious freedom, and it provides:

> That no person or persons whatsoever within this province . . . professing to believe in Jesus Christ, shall from henceforth be any ways troubled, molested or discountenanced for or in respect of his or her religion nor in the free exercise thereof . . . nor any way compelled to the belief or exercise of any other religion against his or her consent, so as they be not unfaithful to the Lord Proprietary, or molest or conspire against the civil government.[8]

This measure does not, however, state in explicit terms that settlers would enjoy liberty of conscience. That the measure was intended for that purpose was noted some thirty years later by the son of the lord proprietor, the third Lord Baltimore. He said that his father had absolute authority to take with him any who wished to settle in the patent, but when it came time to go, few would consent unless he made provision for liberty of conscience:

> Many there were of this sort of people who declared their willingness to go and plant in the province so as they might be at liberty . . . with their respective judgments and consciences, without being subject to any penalties whatever for their so doing, provided the civil peace was preserved. . . . These were the conditions proposed by such as were willing to go and be the first planters of this province, and without the complying with these conditions, in all probability this province had never been planted. . . .[9]

During the Civil War, support of liberty of conscience emerged in Parliament, and this was a valuable aid to the cause of the colonies. As early as 1643 Parliament recognized the rights of conscience as a central issue that needed reforming. This was evident, for example, in the document of December 23, entitled *Considerations*, which called for the preservation of the rights of particular congregations.[10] Those who could not for conscience' sake conform to this and other provisions were free from harassment. At the same time Parliament began to grant patents with the express provision for liberty of conscience. Charles M. Andrews, in his exhaustive study of the colonies, mentions such cases. Writes Andrews,

> Some time before 1645 certain people in Bermuda petitioned Parliament for the privilege of religious freedom and in October, 1645, the House of Lords ordered that they and such others as should join them were to enjoy liberty of their consciences in matters of God's worship without molestation. . . .[11]

Another example of this practice is the one already mentioned by Winthrop, the one granted to William Sayle.

By the 1650's settlements in Maryland, New York, Providence, the Bahamas, Bermuda, and perhaps elsewhere, claimed the right of liberty of conscience as a fundamental article in their form of government. The rise of Oliver Cromwell did not disturb this pattern, and as the Restoration came, the colonies included many communities that had enjoyed liberty of conscience for two decades and more.

As the character of the Restoration religious settlement unfolded in England, undoubtedly many colonials expected a wave of repression to engulf them. In fact that did not happen. Fitful efforts to force some of the colonies to conform to the design of parliamentary religious policy are a matter of record, but these efforts were only part of the picture. During the years of the Restoration the most significant development in the area of colonial religious life was the rapid spread of the claim for liberty of conscience.

King Charles II aided in the preservation and extension of liberty of conscience in the colonies. Colonials, like their brethren in England, read his statement made from Breda, in which he affirmed "a liberty to tender consciences." They also read his statement later that year when he said his subjects would have "liberty of tender consciences, that no man shall be disquieted or called in question for differences of opinion in matters of religion, which do not disturb the public peace." Like dissenters in England, colonials who defended liberty of conscience had good reason to be encouraged during the months after Charles returned to England.[12]

As the policy of Parliament began to unfold in late 1661, however, the story of liberty of conscience took a different pattern in the colonies than it did in England. Despite parliamentary measures, such as the Act of Uniformity, King Charles wrote Governor Berkeley in 1662 the following message:

> Because we are willing to give all possible encouragement to persons of different persuasion in matters of religion to transport themselves thither with their stocks; you are not to suffer any man to be molested or disquieted in the exercise of his religion, so he be content with a quiet and peaceable enjoying it, not giving therein offense or scandal to the government.[13]

In other words, Berkeley was instructed to include liberty of conscience as an article of government.

Following Charles's letter to Berkeley, his support for the cause of liberty of conscience in the colonies continued. The next year he granted a new charter to Rhode Island and Providence Plantations, and it included the following provision:

> Charles The Second. . . .
> That our royal will and pleasure is, that no person within the said colony, at any time hereafter, shall be any wise molested, punished, disquieted, or called into question, for any difference in opinion in any matters of religion, and do not actually disturb the civil peace of our said colony; but that all and every person and persons may . . . at all times hereafter, freely and fully have and enjoy his and their own judgments and consciences, in matters of religious concernments, through the tract of land hereafter mentioned. . . .[14]

In the same year Charles granted a charter to cover the colony of Carolina. In it he made an interesting distinction concerning liberty. After stating that at times people could not conform to the established church, he gave the patentees "full and free license, liberty and authority" to grant "such indulgencies and dispensations" to their settlers as they thought necessary to secure peace and quiet in the colony.[15] He did not thus require liberty of conscience as a condition of the charter. Two years later, however, the patentees published the Concessions and Agreements of the lord proprietors of the Province of Carolina; it included liberty of conscience as a fundamental right. No person at any time was to be molested for differences in opinion and practice in religion; rather, all persons were to enjoy their liberty in judgment and conscience. The patentees added to these provisions the phrase, "custom of this realm of England to the contrary hereof in anywise notwithstanding," the phrase suggesting that they were aware that their practice was a departure from practice in England and elsewhere.[16]

In 1665, the same year the patentees of Carolina issued their Concessions and Agreements, King Charles issued them a new charter, enlarging the grant. Carolina's charter of 1665 contained a verbatim repetition of the clause on liberty of conscience used in the Rhode Island charter of 1663.[17]

The practice of making liberty of conscience a fundamental article in the patents granted during the first years of the Restoration continued throughout the rest of the seventeenth century, even in the more complicated transactions dealing with the middle colonies. The New Jerseys and Pennsylvania all provided for liberty of conscience, and they did so at every stage of their legal development.

The Jersey colonies began their legal development toward separate entities in 1664, when Charles granted his brother, Duke of York, the territory encompassing New York and New Jersey. In a few months James had arranged to convey the New Jersey portion of the grant to two friends, Lord John Berkeley and Sir George Carteret, "in as full and ample manner as the same is granted to the Duke of York."[18] For several decades the meaning of this phrase was not clear, and it clouded the legal development of New Jersey. Meanwhile, Berkeley and Carteret published Concessions and Agreements in an effort to attract settlers, the document being similar to that used by the Carolina settlers. It contained the same clause used in Carolina and Rhode Island on liberty of conscience.[19] As if aware that the title to the territory was in question, the proprietors included an additional provision:

> That no pretense may be taken by our heirs or assigns for or by reason of our right of patronage and power of advouson, granted by his majesty's Letter's Patents, unto his Royal Highness James Duke of York, and by his Royal Highness unto us, thereby to infringe the general clause of liberty of conscience, aforementioned. . . .[20]

From the beginning, thus, the New Jerseys were on the same ground as Rhode Island and Carolina concerning liberty of conscience.

Soon after the Concessions and Agreements was published, New Jersey experienced a steady influx of settlers, some from New England who tended to reside in the northern part of the territory, and others, largely Quakers, who settled in the southern part of New Jersey. While there were undoubtedly many reasons why these people came into New Jersey, many of them came because of the assurance provided by the Concession, that they would be able to enjoy liberty of conscience.

New Jersey, however, was to become two separate colonies as a result of Lord Berkeley's sale of his interest in 1674 to two Quakers, John Fenwick and Edward Byllinge. The separation occurred in 1676 through conveyance by deed, Carteret becoming sole proprietor of what was called East Jersey, and a group of Quakers emerging as co-proprietors of West Jersey. The next year the proprietors of West Jersey issued the Fundamental Laws of West Jersey as part of their Concessions and Agreements, and it provided for liberty of conscience.[21]

At the time the Concession was issued, a dispute arose between the claim of the proprietors and Governor Andros of New York, the latter claiming that he controlled New Jersey. This precluded the meeting of a provincial assembly as provided for in the Concession. Such an assembly met, however, in 1681, and one of its first items of business was the enactment of "fundamentals" which were to be inviolable in the province. This document follows closely the form set down in the Concession of 1677. One student of constitutional history suggests that the laws of 1681 reflect numerous rights which the

Whig party in England was struggling to secure.[22] As for liberty of conscience, the language of 1681 guaranteeing it to the inhabitants of West Jersey was much more succinct than it was in earlier expressions in New Jersey. The document of 1681 read, in Article Ten, "That liberty of conscience in matters of faith and worship toward God shall be granted to all people within the Province aforesaid, who shall live peaceable and quietly therein. . . ." East Jersey followed the same pattern two years later.[23]

The story of William Penn and the founding of the colony named for his father is one always treated at length in colonial histories, and religious liberty as a basic motive for the founding of the colony receives prominent attention. The religious liberty provision in colonial Pennsylvania was based upon Penn's belief in and devotion to liberty of conscience. His Frame of Government of 1682, and the revision of it the next year, evidence this position.[24] The Pennsylvania Charter of Privileges of 1701, Penn's final restatement of the basic laws, also made provision for liberty of conscience. It is worth noting, not only as a matter of simple evidence, but also because it shows how liberty of conscience fit into Penn's general philosophy of political and social institutions:

> Because no People can be truly happy, though under the greatest Enjoyment of Civil Liberties, if abridged of the Freedom of their Consciences, as to their Religious Profession and Worship: And Almighty God being the only Lord of Conscience. Father of Lights and Spirits; and the Author as well as Object of all divine Knowledge, Faith and Worship, who only doth enlighten the Minds, and persuade and convince the Understandings of People. I do hereby grant and declare, That no Person or Persons, inhabiting in this Province or Territories, who shall confess and acknowledge One almighty God, the Creator, Upholder and Ruler of the World; and profess him or themselves obliged to live quietly under the Civil Government, shall be in any Case molested or prejudiced, in his or their Person or Estate, because of his or their conscientious Persuasion or Practice, nor be compelled to frequent or maintain any religious Worship, Place or Ministry, contrary to his or their Mind, or to do or suffer any other Act or Thing, contrary to their religious Persuasion.[25]

Pennsylvania operated under this charter until 1776.

By 1689, or by 1701 if Penn's revised charter be included, the rights of conscience were established in the basic laws of most of the colonies. These institutional expressions of the rights of conscience were significant, not only for the protection they afforded those who lived under them during the colonial era, but also because these provisions continued into the eighteenth century until the time when the new states adopted new constitutions. These provisions provide continuous testimony to the cause of conscience and its liberty from the earliest days of settlement until the time of the Revolution.

During the period 1630-1689 many individuals also expressed their devotion to liberty of conscience. Noted in an earlier chapter were the views of Roger Williams and Anne Hutchinson. The townsmen of Providence individually spoke for the cause of liberty of conscience as they signed their new town charter in 1640. Later, as the Quakers migrated to the middle colonies, and as they attempted to invade Massachusetts Bay Colony, they argued for liberty of conscience, a point that has been documented in great detail by the Quaker historian, Rufus Jones.

Viewing the period 1630-1689 as a whole, it is obvious that liberty of conscience in the American colonies was accepted as a basic principle of institutional and social life by many people, the position of Massachusetts Bay Colony being an obvious exception. Cognizant of these developments, particularly of the provisions for liberty of conscience in the charters and other laws of the colonies, examination of the problem of liberty of conscience during the period 1689-1770 may be better understood.

B. *Liberty, Sovereignty, and Revolutionary Ideology: 1689-1770*

While the charters and other legal provisions for liberty of conscience continued throughout the rest of the colonial period, it became apparent by 1689 that liberty of conscience was increasingly important in the formation of an emerging American political ideology. This development may be seen in two ways: in the day-to-day discussions of interested persons, and in the writings of John Locke, who has long been recognized as influential in the formation of American political ideas. To maintain a proper perspective on these developments it will be useful to focus on Locke first, thereafter noting the familiarity with the ideas of liberty and sovereignty as they have been set forth in this study.

Since the publication of Carl Becker's *Declaration of Independence* in 1922, there has been a sustained interest in the role of Locke in the formation of American Revolutionary ideology.[26] Becker laid to rest the long-standing idea that Rousseau was the pre-eminent force behind Revolutionary ideas; and at the same time he raised to Rousseau's vacant seat the Englishman John Locke. In speaking of Locke's influence Becker said, "Jefferson copied Locke."[27] Subsequently, writers such as Bernard Bailyn have modified Becker's view, suggesting that Lockean ideas came to America earlier, and largely through the writings of English Opposition authors in the early years of the eighteenth century.[28] Lawrence Leder, in his recent study of liberty and authority during the period 1689-1763, also recognized the influence of Locke. In speaking of the approaches to the problem of the origin and purpose of government set forth by a variety of colonial writers, he concluded that they "ensconced Lockean theory firmly in the American mind."[29] Elsewhere Leder speaks of "the general enthusiasm for Lockean theory" among colonials.[30]

Locke thus has long been recognized as a potent source of ideas for the development of American political ideology, but the question of which Lockean ideas were important in America needs to be looked at in some detail. Locke has often been pictured as fostering a natural rights philosophy, and certain of his writings comment on this problem.[31] Locke's speculative views on the question of the state of nature prior to the formation of societies has also been pointed out.[32] Still other writers have discussed his view of property and its relationship to government.[33] There can be no doubt about the fact that these ideas were current in America in the years after 1689; and there can be no doubt about the fact that, in certain cases, the expressions in America were gleaned from Locke.

Locke, however, also had specific views about liberty of conscience and sphere sovereignty, though this has not often been recognized. What Locke said about these ideas deserves special attention here because his comments on them were echoed frequently in American political ideology in the period after 1689.

Studies by Alan Heimert[34] and Staunton Lynd[35] both point out that Locke's *Letter on Toleration*[36] was a popular item in eighteenth-century America, and odd though it may seem at first glance, this letter is, in fact, a detailed comment on liberty and sovereignty in the tradition of Perkins and the Westminster Assembly. This essay was written a few months before its publication in 1689, the same year that the Toleration Act passed into law. The appearance of Locke's letter and the Act in the same year are purely a matter of coincidence. Locke's use of this word in the letter makes it clear that he did not conceive of it in the same way that it had been used for generations by governmental officials, the way that it was used in the Act. Locke used the word *toleration* in the sense of Christian charity, a point that is obvious in the letter itself.

The letter was labeled with the word *toleration* for the simple reason that someone had written to him to ask what his views were on the subject, reference to this query being made in the first lines of the letter.[37] But Locke did not stop with a passing comment on toleration as Christian charity; he took the occasion to illustrate what it should be, also giving examples where it was absent. Subsequently he went on to state his view of liberty and sovereignty. That he lingered over the problem of Christian charity is a clue to his view of how it is that men ought to live together, of what conditions ought to prevail if true liberty and sovereignty are to be possible.

As for Christian charity, he began discussing it with several illustrations of situations in which it was absent. Said Locke, Christians may boast of tradition, as the Anglicans did; they may boast of reforming zeal or of orthodoxy, as some Puritans did; but these are not the marks of the Christian and his church. These are marks of "men striving for power and empire over one another."[38] Locke had no objection to tradition *per se;* yet if a man "be destitute of charity, meekness, and good will in general toward all mankind, even to those who are not Christians, he is certainly yet short of being a true Christian himself."[39] In this Locke sets the tone of what he means by *toleration,* and he reinforces his view by appeal to Scripture: "If the Gospel and the apostles may be credited, no man can be a Christian without charity, and without faith which works, not by force, but by love."[40]

To drive his point home, to make it clear that Christian charity was "the chief characteristic mark of the true church,"[41] Locke gave an example of a situation in which this spirit was absent. "Now I appeal to the consciences of those who persecute, torment, destroy, and kill other men upon pretense of religion, whether they do it out of friendship and kindness towards them or no?"[42] Locke will believe them when he sees them treating their close friends with the same vigor. Persecutors are lax, says Locke, for they wink at "whoredom, fraud, malice and such like enormities, which according to the apostle manifestly relish of heathenism."[43] These, says Locke,

> ... are certainly more contrary to the glory of God to the purity of the church, and to the salvation of souls, than any *conscientious* dissent from ecclesiastical decisions, or separation from public worship, whilst accompanied with innocence of life.[44]

Persecution of innocent dissent while obvious vices go unchecked is a way to build a Christian church that to Locke "is altogether incredible."

In contrast to this situation, Locke suggests how it is that church leaders and magistrates should conduct themselves if they have Christian charity, and follow the rule of Scripture:

> If, like the Captain of our salvation, they sincerely desired the good of souls, they would tread in the steps and follow the perfect example of that Prince of Peace, who sent out His soldiers to the subduing of nations, and gathering them into His Church, not armed with the sword or other instruments of force, but prepared with the Gospel of peace with exemplary holiness of their conversation. This was His method.[45]

Further, Locke notes that the Prince of Peace could have provided that the gospel be spread by force, rather than by persuasion; but if that had been His intention, "we know very well that it was much more easy for Him to do it with armies of heavenly legions than for any son of the church, however potent."[46]

Toleration or Christian charity, for Locke, is thus the chief mark of the Christian. It is essential because the spread of the gospel and the salvation of souls depend upon it. This stance avoids force and coercion in dealing with men; instead, it depends upon peace and kindness, and persuasion by examples of holiness.

Christian charity was not, however, an end in itself for Locke; rather, it was only one facet of Locke's belief that religion was the "highest obligation that lies upon mankind."[47] *Religion* was the word Locke used to describe how man as creature related to God as Creator:

> Every man has an immortal soul, capable of eternal happiness or misery, whose happiness depends upon his believing and doing those things in this life which are necessary to the obtaining of God's favor, and are prescribed by God to that end.[48]

Believing that "there is nothing in this world that is of any consideration in comparison with eternity," Locke went on to say that "the care of each man's salvation belongs only to himself."[49] In this context Locke's observation that no life lived "against the *dictates of his conscience* will ever bring him to the mansions of the blessed"[50] is most significant. Stated another way, if a person lives continuously in violation of his conscience, he is sure to be damned. In this, Locke places conscience at the center of religion, and thus at the center of a person's life. In another passage of the letter he makes the same point when he writes that religious opinions belong "entirely to the *conscience* of every particular man, for the conduct of which he is accountable to God only."[51] In other words, echoing the Westminster Confession, God alone is Lord of the conscience and has made it free from the doctrines and commandments of men.

Since religion is the "highest obligation" that lies on any man and since the fulfillment of that obligation is "entirely" a matter of conscience for which he is "accountable to God only," Locke appears to promote the liberty and sovereignty of the individual. As could be expected, like other advocates of liberty of conscience before him, Locke identifies other spheres, particularly those of church and state, and, in the context of liberty of conscience and sphere sovereignty, attempts to define their limits. Wrote Locke,

> I esteem it above all things necessary to distinguish exactly the

business of civil government from that of [organized] religion, and to settle the just bounds that lie between the one and the other.[52]

This was essential:

> If this be not done, there can be no end put to the controversies that will be always arising between those that have, or at least pretend to have, on the one side, a concernment for the interest of men's souls, and, on the other side, a care for the commonwealth.[53]

Government is a separate sphere of jurisdiction, and the scope of its power covers the commonwealth, the latter being "a society of men constituted only for the procuring, preserving, and advancing of their own civil interests." Civil interests consist of "life, liberty, health . . . and the possession of outward things, such as money, lands, houses, furniture, and the like."[54] The magistrate, as a creature of the civil government, has a duty "by impartial execution of the laws, to secure unto all the people in general, and to every one of his subjects in particular, the just possession of these things belonging to this life."[55] To this end the magistrate is armed.

Locke wants it understood that "the whole jurisdiction of the magistrate reaches only to these civil concernments," that it does not involve the salvation of souls. Care of souls "is not committed unto him, I say, by God, because it appears not that God has ever given such authority to one man over another, as to compel anyone to his religion."[56] From another angle, Locke argues that religion is a matter of "inward persuasion of the mind. . . . And such is the nature of the understanding that it cannot be compelled to the belief of anything by outward force."[57]

Next Locke discusses the character of the jurisdiction that fell to organized religion, that is, the church. Unlike many earlier writers, Locke saw the voluntary character of churches as a significant aspect, as one that pointed to its limited jurisdiction. In his words,

> A church, then, I take to be a voluntary society of men, joining themselves together of their own accord in order to the public worshipping of God in such manner as they judge acceptable to Him, and effectual to the salvation of their souls.[58]

If anyone should wonder why it was a voluntary organization, Locke suggested they consider alternative views. For example, if someone was born into the church, he would hold his faith by tenure, inheriting it from his parents. To Locke, that would be absurd. The hope of salvation, says Locke, is the only reason to belong to a church.

The purpose of the church was public worship and the salvation of souls, and, says Locke, it should be run according to the rules "as the Holy Spirit has in the Holy Scriptures declared, in express words, to be necessary to salvation."[59] If churches conduct themselves in this manner, Locke has no doubt that they would serve the needs of men. Churches were after all made for men, not men for the churches. Locke concludes his discussion of the character of jurisdiction that fell to churches by stating that "nothing ought nor can be transacted in this society relating to the possession of civil and worldly goods."[60]

To the ears of advocates of much churchly power and authority Locke's view of the church as a modest organization with a circumscribed area of jurisdiction could be construed as an abdication of responsibility toward society and its morality. Such a conclusion could be made if his view of conscience was not fully understood and appreciated. The fact is that his limiting of the power and authority that fell to the government and churches required a high view of conscience and its liberty. Man as a religious being might belong to a church, but that did not relieve him of his responsibility to live according to the dictates of his conscience. The same was true concerning his membership in a society under a government.

Conscience was normative for man, no matter what institutions he be associated with, this being clear in Locke's discussion of the problem of government and morality. Locke recognized the magistrate's interest in public morality, and that he had authority to enforce it. This authority was, however, limited to obvious and universally accepted evils, such as murder. When individual consciences came into conflict with public morality and the government's interest in it, Locke had no reservations in stating:

> Everyone should do what he in his conscience is persuaded to be acceptable to the Almighty, on whose good pleasure and accept-

ance their eternal happiness depends. For observance is due, in the first place to God, and afterward to the laws.[61]

Here Locke brings together a number of points he had made earlier, namely, that conscience is normative in man's relationship to God, that the latter is man's highest concern, and that the jurisdiction of the government is limited.

Locke illustrates this position with two examples, one in which the magistrate requires a deed that appears to the conscience as unlawful, and a second in which the magistrate requires something that does not fall within his jurisdiction. In the first case Locke refers to a situation in which the person judges something to be unlawful to his conscience, such as objection to a given war. Locke felt that in a well-run society such a situation would seldom exist, because the magistrate would always seek the peace and quiet of his subjects. Should it happen, however, Locke says, "A private person is to abstain from the action that he judges unlawful, and he is to undergo the punishment which it is not *unlawful* for him to bear."[62] It is worth noting in passing that Locke suggests that some punishment is unlawful, and ought not to be accepted.

As for the case in which the magistrate requires something not within his jurisdiction, Locke says, "Men are not in these cases obliged by that law, against their consciences." If it be objected that the magistrate believe he is doing good, Locke again speaks without equivocation:

> The private judgment (as I may call it) of the magistrate does not give him any new right of imposing laws upon his subjects which neither was in the constitution of the government granted him nor was ever in the power of the people to grant.[63]

Again Locke reflects his conception of separate spheres of activity and how it is that they are related to conscience. Even if the situation arise in which a conflict between the individual and the government cannot be reconciled, Locke has no doubt that the person should follow his conscience. Like St. Paul and many later writers, Locke pointed out that in the end God will judge each and reward each according to his desire to promote peace and the other Christian virtues. In the meantime, the individual should care for "his own soul first, and in the next place . . . public peace."⁶⁴ Caring for one's soul required adherence to the dictates of conscience, for, as Locke said earlier, no one could expect to enter the mansions of the blessed without following the rule of conscience.

Locke concluded his letter with a prayer or benediction in which he touched the high points of his argument:

> God Almighty grant, I beseech Him, that the gospel of peace may at length be preached, and that the civil magistrates, growing more careful to conform their consciences to the law of God and less solicitous about the binding of other men's consciences by human laws, may, like fathers of their country, direct all their counsels and endeavors to promote universally the civil welfare of all their children, except only of such as are arrogant, ungovernable, and injurious to their brethren; and that all ecclesiastical men, who boast themselves to be successors of the apostles, walking peaceably and modestly in the apostles' steps, without intermeddling with state affairs, may apply themselves wholly to promote the salvation of souls.⁶⁵

From the foregoing it is clear that John Locke advocated the same view of conscience and sovereignty that had been set forth by a variety of writers since the days of William Perkins. For him conscience must be at liberty, because it is only then that man can care for the most important business he has in this life, namely, the salvation of his soul. Conscience is normative in defining the spheres of authority that fall to government and the church, too, for while each of these institutions has its lawful duties, it does not extend to the concerns of conscience of the individual. Finally, Locke's discussion of liberty and sovereignty in the context of Christian charity is noteworthy because it reflects his conviction that liberty of conscience is an idea that ought to be fostered above all by Christians.

Placing Locke in the tradition of Perkins and other Puritans may grate on the historical image of Locke that has appeared in many accounts of the man and his ideas. A comment or two on Locke, the man, therefore, is in order. The usual image of Locke pictures him as an urbane gentleman on the order of a Ben Franklin. It would be more accurate, however, to see him as a representative of later English Puritanism; at least this conclusion may be drawn from a recent study of his letters and journals, items that have become available only in the last twenty years.⁶⁶ Locke's continuous association with men like John Owen also suggests that he was familiar with, and to a degree the product of, the Puritan movement in England. In conclusion concerning Locke, it may be said that his works yield many new insights when he is read without the tinted glass of modern secularism.

During the period 1689-1770 the cause of conscience and its liberty in America had both a practical and a theoretical foundation. The charters and other laws continued in force, and, at the same time, Locke's views were being circulated. Not everyone read Locke, but as will be evident, many advocates of liberty and sovereignty either cited him as their authority or borrowed his words and phrases *in toto*. In addition to the charter provisions and the writings of Locke, Americans during the period drew upon the Westminster Confession and other earlier expressions on liberty and sovereignty in the tradition of William Perkins as they defended the rights of the individual and the need for separation of church and state.

In turning to a discussion of the day-to-day use of the ideas of liberty and sovereignty during the period of 1689-1770, it is apparent that many American colonials were concerned about the relationship between individuals and institutions, particularly between individuals and government. The concept of sphere sovereignty was often employed in disputes between advocates of governmental authority and those who saw its authority as limited. A few of these disputes may be cited to demonstrate the manner in which sphere sovereignty was employed.

A Philadelphia businessman, for example, proposed the publication of a newspaper, and the question of libel at common law had been an issue that concerned many people. From another perspective, the question of the limits of the liberty of the press were in the process of being defined. The publisher's prospectus commented on this problem and assured the public that it did not intend to contribute to "the licentiousness of the press." In this the publisher obviously recognized that all liberty had limits.⁶⁷ On the other hand, he made it clear that governmental authority was bounded within a definable jurisdiction. In the words of the prospectus:

> We are commanded to pay obedience to governors, yet not to all generally, but only to those who use their authority for the punishment of evildoers and for the praise of those that do well. ... Where the end of government is perverted, it is criminal in any man to acquiesce under it.[68]

In other words, this publisher was stating that the business of government did not extend to his paper, that the government's sphere of authority did not encompass regulation of the press. His recognition, however, that the liberty of the press had limits was consistent with his view of sphere sovereignty, the question of the limits of liberty always being a part of the dispute when jurisdiction came into conflict.

Thomas Maule's *Tribute to Caesar, How Paid by the Best Christians*, written in 1712, displays the same devotion to liberty and sovereignty. Men gathered themselves into societies, wrote Maule, so "that they might live safely and enjoy their liberties."[69] This liberty could be enjoyed, however, only when the spheres of government and the church were clearly marked off and observed. "Civil societies have their laws proper and peculiar to themselves, and the churches have their rules of discipline peculiar to themselves," said Maule. Further, when the civil magistrates and the church "confound their *jurisdictions* under the law," confusion and conflicts can be the only result.[70] Maule sought to distinguish exactly the business of government and of church, and, to borrow the words of Locke, "settle the just bounds that lie between the one and the other."

Samuel Willard, known to students of New England for his summary of Christian doctrine, preached an election sermon in 1694 that reflects his commitment to sphere sovereignty. Government was ordained by God, says Willard, "to prevent and cure disorders that are apt to break forth among the societies of men; and to promote the civil peace and prosperity of such a people."[71] For Willard the purpose of government was the same as stated by Locke, and earlier by the Westminster Divines. "Government is God's ordinance; and those that are vested with it . . . have their authority from Him," says Willard. While rulers have their authority from God, it must be emphasized, according to Willard, that "people are not made for rulers, but rulers for a people."[72] In this Willard reflects a commitment to the conception of sovereignty that has been outlined in this study.

Another example of devotion to the tradition of liberty and sovereignty may be found in the writings of John Wise. Man, according to Wise, was a "freeborn subject under the crown of heaven," and he owed "homage to none but God himself." God "provided a rule for men in all their actions," and it is found "in the soul of man."[73] In other words, God alone is Lord of man and has given him a guide within himself that must be followed in his actions that relate to other men and institutions.

While some writers during the period 1689-1770 stressed the concept of sphere sovereignty, others appealed directly to liberty of conscience as they defended individual rights over against other men and institutions. The following examples were drawn from a large number of such expressions, and an attempt has been made to use examples from the different colonies over the whole time span being examined.

A Rhode Islander displayed a deft sense of history when he contrasted the atmosphere in early Massachusetts with that of his colony. People in seventeenth-century Rhode Island, as now, he wrote, enjoyed "liberty of conscience, which is freedom to worship God in the way we are persuaded is most agreeable to His will and most acceptable to Him."[74] Liberty of conscience is freedom from interference by other men and institutions. With an eye to developments at the time of the Revolution, his further comment that liberty of conscience "is the only *indefeasible* right of all men,"[75] is significant. His use of *indefeasible* here is the sense that others, at the time of the Revolution, tried to convey when they spoke of rights as unalienable. Liberty of conscience for this writer was a right that could not be trampled upon or taken away by any person or institution.

Peter Clark, in a Boston election sermon, speaking on the question of the relationship between the government and religion, borrowed heavily from the Westminster Confession. Said Clark of the magistrate:

... [He] may not use his authority to impose articles of faith or modes of worship on the consciences of the subjects, or enforce these by civil penalties; for the consciences of men are immediately subject to God, and acknowledge no superior but Him alone.[76]

In other words, God alone was Lord of the conscience and had set it free from the authority of men. Clark not only saw conscience as free from the authority of men, but suggested, as did Locke, that the magistrate had a duty to see that liberty of conscience was not violated by other men and institutions. When liberty of conscience was allowed to be trampled upon, Clark stated, "the sacred ligaments of society and government are at once broken and dissolved."[77] For Clark, liberty of conscience was the normative factor in the proper operation of society, for it was the backbone of the concept of sphere sovereignty, a concept that posited a limited jurisdiction to the spheres of church and state.

Charles Chauncy, a leading figure in theological circles, spoke of liberty of conscience in terms that echo Locke. Said Chauncy, "The use of force in matters of religion and conscience is not only contrary to the example of Christ . . . but to the nature and reason of things." Force in matters of conscience is "a method altogether unsuited to work upon the minds of men. For whatever influence it might have upon their bodies, it can have none upon their souls."[78]

In Pennsylvania liberty of conscience, provided for in the charter, was often used as a defense against government action. During a period when the governor, George Thomas, sought to raise money for the militia, a number of Quakers objected. Thomas found it necessary to assure these Quakers that he, too, believed in liberty of conscience. Said Thomas,

> Far be it from me to attempt the least invasion of your charter, or your laws for liberty of conscience, or to engage any assembly in measures that may introduce persecution for conscience sake. I have always been a professed advocate for liberty, both civil and religious, as the only rational foundation of society.[79]

Thomas here views liberty of conscience as the very foundation of society. Liberty of conscience is the normative factor in defining the just bounds that separate the jurisdiction that falls to the government and other institutions.

Liberty of conscience also played a part in the defense of the right to private judgment and principles, this being evident in a Pennsylvania magazine. The writer began by inquiring whether the men of the Reformation were correct in following their consciences as they split the Church of Rome. If they were right in following their consciences, and if they were correct in resisting attempts to coerce them, then "every man, in every age and nation, hath an equal claim to the same liberty." From this premise the writer went on to say:

> Every Christian hath an equal right to the peaceable and constant possession of his own principles, and ought to be left by all men, and secured by civil government, in the full and undisturbed enjoyment of them.

Moreover, he continued,

> Every Christian hath a further right, to publish and vindicate by reason and argument his own opinions; to speak freely against all corruption of religion . . . to separate from such communions and societies of Christians whose doctrines and worship he cannot in conscience approve of.[80]

Again, as in the examples cited above, the writer here uses the idea of conscience and its liberty to support his view that men are free from the intrusions of institutions and other men.

Another writer in Pennsylvania at about the same time wrote an essay on the right of private judgment, and he links private judgment to liberty of conscience. As in the case just noted, the actions of men of the Reformation were cited as justification for the claim that a Christian should stand on liberty of conscience. The argument that the rights of conscience were the basis of the Reformation was emphasized. Attempts to violate conscience by government or churches or other persons were, said the writer, "unnatural, inhuman, and anti-Christian." The right of private judgment through conscience was one of those "sacred and original rights of human nature which the Gospel had revived and re-established."[81] Further, the rights of conscience were equal in all men, and each man had to account for his actions through conscience. For this reason liberty of conscience was an important and vital concern of society. Finally the writer noted, "A man may alienate his labor, his estate, and several other branches of his property . . . but he cannot transfer his right of conscience," and, he adds with a touch of irony, "unless he could . . . substitute another to be judged for him at the righteous tribunal of God" in the final Day of Judgment.[82]

Noteworthy in these remarks is the idea stated two centuries earlier by William Perkins that liberty of conscience was linked to the gospel, or as in Perkins' words, "Christ hath now in the New Testament given a liberty to conscience."[83] Again this writer noted that conscience and its liberty was something that could not be *alienated*, or transferred.

Liberty of conscience was a prominent argument in New York at the time King's College was being established. Some saw its establishment as a further extension of the Anglican Church, and so they resisted it. One writer likened the occasion to that of French Protestants, and concluded:

> The civil magistrate's power reaches only to the punishing of men for actions detrimental to civil society, not for opinions. Whilst men desire only liberty to worship God according to the dictates of their conscience, and in all other matters are willing to submit to the known laws of the land, no prince that values his reputation . . . will make a new law to entrap such men and bring them under the denomination of rebels.[84]

Concerned also with the threat associated with the establishment of King's College, another writer pointed out that in England there were two traditions of religion, one associated with the Church of England and the other with the Church of Scotland. The point was that there was no unity in England and that it could not be expected in the colonies. The alternative was liberty, and liberty was an inviolable right of men. As for the source of liberty in general, it was tied to liberty of conscience. Liberty of conscience "cannot be transferred; it claims an entire exemption from human jurisdiction, because its ends, offices, and interests are superior to all the ends of civil association."[85] Significantly the writer adds that if the government tries to usurp this right, it degenerates into tyranny, and the right of self-defense must be exercised. In short, liberty of conscience is the basis of other liberties, and when it is attacked, the solution is self-defense, or revolution.

By mid-century an essay in a Connecticut paper pointed out that the colony's college had been founded "upon principles of liberty of conscience," and it was the same liberty of conscience that dissenters from the English Church had fought for.[86] The point of the essay was summed up in the phrase, "Our forefathers enjoyed liberty of conscience; shall we give it up?"[87]

By 1760 the cause of conscience and its liberty had advanced throughout the colonies, even in Massachusetts. One advocate argued:

> The civil government as they exercise their authority to rule only in temporary things are the ministers of God . . . . God hath not committed to them the government of his church, or to meddle in cases of conscience.[88]

Another wrote:

> The right of private judgment is inalienable—and since it is essential to true religion that we act from conscience and a conviction that what we profess and practice is agreeable to the divine will—religious liberty ever supposes, and it is requisite to its being, that the conscience be left free and that none pretend to an empire over it.[89]

An election sermon of 1762 by Abraham Williams sums up the view that prevailed at the time of the Revolution. Williams said,

> Human laws cannot control the mind—the rights of conscience are unalienable; inseparable from our nature—they ought not, they cannot possibly be given up to society. Therefore religion, as it consists in right sentiments, affections, and behavior towards God—as it is chiefly internal and private, can be regulated only by God himself.[90]

Concluding this point Williams stated that civil authority had a right to encourage public worship, but only if it was "consistent with an entire liberty of conscience."[91]

During the period 1689-1770 American colonials often drew

upon the idea of conscience and its liberty to defend individual rights against real or imagined encroachments by the government. Liberty of conscience could be adapted to the problem of the freedom of the press, as well as to other areas of individual freedom. In this it contributed to the growing appreciation of the difference between English governmental conceptions of individual rights and a distinctively American one. As one writer put it, "Americans reverenced liberty" in the eighteenth century. Applying this observation to the Revolution, he continued, "American goals remained unchanged" throughout the century; hence, "Americans confidently entered the struggle with Britain over the meaning and extent of liberty."[92]

Often the question of church and state entered the political arena during this period, and often colonials argued for their separation in terms of sphere sovereignty based upon conscience and its liberty. On this question, as regarding those that affected the individual more directly, the colonials quoted, paraphrased, and alluded to earlier expressions on liberty and sovereignty in the tradition of William Perkins. Among the more obvious sources for the colonials were the views of John Locke and the Westminster Confession of Faith, though some colonials spoke as though they had copies of Perkins' treatises on their reference shelves.

While the range of persons who cited liberty of conscience during the period 1689-1770 was no doubt greater than it was during the earlier phases of seventeenth-century colonial experience, the two periods are integrally related. The review of charter provisions for liberty of conscience during the various stages of settlement indicates a firm commitment to the idea. Moreover, individuals during the early period in most of the colonies frequently expressed their devotion to liberty of conscience. The charters themselves provided continuity throughout the period, for they remained in force until superseded by constitutional provisions in the new states. The period 1689-1770 may be distinguished from the earlier phase in that it experienced a quickening of interest in the argument from conscience for sphere sovereignty and individual liberty, this phenomenon contributing to an emerging American political ideology.

In sum then, concerning liberty of conscience in colonial America, it may be said that the idea arrived early and soon became a basic principle in most of the colonial charters, Massachusetts Bay Colony being the outstanding exception. Further, by the end of the seventeenth century, liberty and sovereignty became important elements in an emerging political ideology. Finally, as the argument from conscience and its liberty became more popular as an element in political ideology, it reflected a debt to John Locke, the Westminster Confession, and others in the tradition of William Perkins. As the Revolution approached in the 1770's, liberty of conscience was an important principle, one that Americans were ready and willing to guarantee as they created their new instruments of government.

CHAPTER NOTES

1. *Supra*, chap. III.
2. Winthrop, *Journal*, I, p. 28.
3. *Ibid.*, II, p. 257.
4. *Ibid.*, pp. 251-252.
5. *Ibid.*, p. 307.
6. F. N. Thorpe, *The Federal and State Constitutions, Colonial Charters, and Other Organic Laws* (Washington, 1909), VI, pp. 3205-3207; hereinafter cited as Thorpe, *Constitutions*.
7. Rufus M. Jones, *The Quakers in the American Colonies* (New York, 1966), p. 272.
8. William H. Brown, ed., *Archives of Maryland* (Baltimore, 1883), I, p. 246.
9. Quoted in George Petrie, *Church and State in Early Maryland* (Baltimore, 1892), pp. 195-196.
10. Quoted by C. M. Andrews in *The Colonial Period of American History* (New Haven, 1934, 1964), IV, p. 494, note.
11. *Ibid.*
12. *Supra*, p. 109.
13. Jones, *Quakers*, p. 272.
14. Thorpe, *Constitutions*, VI, p. 3211 ff.
15. *Ibid.*, V, p. 2747.
16. *Ibid.*, p. 2757.
17. *Ibid.*, p. 2771.
18. *Ibid.*, p. 2534.
19. *Ibid.*
20. *Ibid.*
21. *Ibid.*

22. E. P. Tanner, *The Province of New Jersey, 1664-1738* (New York, 1908), p. 113 ff.
23. Thorpe, *Constitutions*, V, p. 2565 ff.
24. *Ibid.*, pp. 3035-3044.
25. *Ibid.*, pp. 3076-3081.
26. Carl Becker, *The Declaration of Independence* (New York, 1922).
27. *Ibid.*, p. 278.
28. Bernard Bailyn, *The Ideological Origins of the American Revolution* (Cambridge, 1967).
29. Lawrence Leder, *Liberty and Authority: Early American Political Ideology 1689-1763* (Chicago, 1968), p. 39; hereinafter cited as Leder, *Liberty*.
30. *Ibid.*, p. 42.
31. Staughton Lynd, *The Intellectual Origins of American Radicalism* (New York, 1968), p. 20 ff.; hereinafter cited as Lynd, *Radicalism*.
32. Leder, *Liberty*, p. 37 ff.
33. Lynd, *Radicalism*, p. 34 ff.
34. Alan Heimert, *Religion and the American Mind: From the Great Awakening to the Revolution* (Cambridge, 1966), p. 17.
35. Lynd, *Radicalism*, p. 27.
36. Locke wrote four letters on toleration. The first one, written in 1688-1689, is by far the most famous one, going through dozens of editions. The title of this letter varies. I have used John Locke, *A Letter Concerning Toleration*, Patrick Romanell, ed. (New York, 1955); hereinafter cited as Locke, *Letter*.
37. *Ibid.*, p. 13.
38. *Ibid.*
39. *Ibid.*
40. *Ibid.*, p. 14.
41. *Ibid.*
42. *Ibid.*
43. *Ibid.*
44. *Ibid.* (italics mine).
45. *Ibid.*, p. 16.
46. *Ibid.*
47. *Ibid.*, p. 46.
48. *Ibid.*
49. *Ibid.*
50. *Ibid.*, p. 34 (italics mine).
51. *Ibid.*, p. 58 (italics mine).
52. Locke, *Letter*, p. 17.
53. *Ibid.*
54. *Ibid.*
55. *Ibid.*

56. *Ibid.*, p. 18.
57. *Ibid.*
58. *Ibid.*, p. 20.
59. *Ibid.*, p. 22.
60. *Ibid.*, pp. 22, 23.
61. *Ibid.*, p. 48.
62. *Ibid.* (italics mine).
63. *Ibid.*, p. 49.
64. *Ibid.*
65. *Ibid.*, p. 59.
66. Maurice Cranston, *John Locke: A Biography* (New York, 1957).
67. Leder, *Liberty*, p. 30.
68. *Ibid.*
69. Thomas Maule, *Tribute to Caesar* (Philadelphia, 1712), p. 12.
70. *Ibid.* (italics mine).
71. Leder, *Liberty*, p. 46.
72. *Ibid.*
73. John Wise, *A Vindication of the Government of the New England Churches* (Boston, 1717), pp. 33-38.
74. *Rhode Island Gazette*, January 11, 1733/34.
75. *Ibid.* (italics mine).
76. Peter Clark, *The Rulers Highest Dignity, and the Peoples Truest Glory* (Boston, 1739), pp. 18-19.
77. *Ibid.*
78. Charles Chauncy, *The Only Compulsion Proper to be Made Use of in the Affairs of Conscience and Religion* (Boston, 1739), p. 9.
79. *American Weekly Mercury*, January 15, 1739/40.
80. *Ibid.*, January 20, 1743/44.
81. *Pennsylvania Gazette*, January 19, 1947/48.
82. *Ibid.*
83. *Supra*, p. 4.
84. *New York Gazette*, February 12, 1753.
85. *Occasional Reverberator*, October 5, 1753.
86. *Connecticut Gazette*, October 15, 1757.
87. *Ibid.*
88. John Bolles, *To Worship God in Spirit, and in Truth, Is to Worship Him in True Liberty of Conscience* (Boston, 1756), pp. 60-61.
89. Benjamin Stevens, *A Sermon Preached at Boston* (Boston, 1761), p. 11.
90. Abraham Williams, *A Sermon Preached at Boston* (Boston, 1762), p. 10.
91. *Ibid.*
92. Leder, *Liberty*, pp. 19-20.

Chapter VII

LIBERTY OF CONSCIENCE IN THE AMERICAN REVOLUTION

On August 20, 1789, the House of Representatives voted to approve the following provision as an amendment to the Constitution, "Congress shall make no law establishing religion, or to prevent the free exercise thereof, or to infringe the rights of conscience."[1] This provision was designed to quiet the fears of many concerning the future of liberty of conscience, fears that emerged as a result of power given to the new federal government by the new Constitution. Many men in the Congress recognized the need to protect the rights of conscience from an invasion by the new creature which the Constitution created, but it was James Madison who spelled out why it was that this protection was needed.

In the Constitutional Convention and in congressional debates, opponents of a bill of rights in any form frequently cited the English Declaration of Rights and the common law as a protection for rights.[2] Madison, however, saw this stance as entirely inadequate for the American situation, particularly as it affected liberty of conscience. When the argument was raised again in the House debates, Madison pointed out what he saw as its greatest weakness. As for the English Declaration of Rights, he said, "The truth is, they have gone no further than to raise a barrier against the power of the Crown"; thus, "the power of the Legislature is left altogether indefinite." Not only that, when the great rights, "trial by jury, freedom of the press, or liberty of conscience, come into question in that body," the invasion of them is resisted by able advocates through appeal to the Magna Carta. But "the Magna Carta does not contain any one provision for security of those rights, respecting which the people of America are most alarmed," the chief among these being "the rights of conscience." Concluding, Madison said, these "choicest privileges of the people," are not only unprotected by the Magna Carta, they "are unguarded in the British Constitution."[3]

The House's proposed amendment to the Constitution and Madison's comments upon it suggest that liberty of conscience was a fundamental right in the thinking of many of his countrymen. There is abundant evidence that liberty of conscience was a basic element in the climate of opinion at the time of the American Revolution.

Traditionally studies of the American Revolutionary period focus on the Declaration of Independence and the federal Constitution with its amendments; but in examining the place of liberty of conscience in the era of the Revolution it will be useful to alter this convention slightly. While the Declaration and the Constitution will be examined in due course, a better perspective on the development of liberty of conscience may be gained through observing a number of state constitutions first. These constitutions are often neglected in studies of the period, but they provide an index of the pervasiveness, if not popularity, of certain ideas, including liberty of conscience.

Once the state constitutions have been examined, attention will be given to the Declaration and the Constitution. Following a survey of all these documents, it will be useful to evaluate the relationship between liberty of conscience as it appeared in the era of the Revolution and the questions of a church establishment in Massachusetts and of the separationist interpretation as it has appeared in the twentieth century.

A. *Liberty and Sovereignty in the Constitutions of the New States*

The Continental Congress in May, 1776, circulated a letter to the states advising them to formulate instruments of government in view of the fact that a decision had been made to publish a declartion of independence.[4] Pursuant to this advice each of the states created constitutions excepting Rhode Island and Connecticut, these two choosing to operate for a time under their old charters.[5] In creating these new constitutions each of the states made specific provision for liberty of conscience, and they did so in terms of sphere sovereignty. To facilitate an examination of these constitutional provisions it will be useful to quote several of them at length.

SEC. 16. That religion, or the duty which we owe to our Creator, and the manner of discharging it, can be directed only by reason and conviction, not by force or violence; and therefore all men are equally entitled to the free exercise of religion, according to the dictates of conscience; and that it is the mutual duty of all to practice Christian forbearance, love, and charity towards each other. Virginia, 1776

II. That all men have a natural and unalienable right to worship Almighty God according to the dictates of their own consciences and understanding: and that no man ought or of right can be compelled to attend any religious worship, or erect or support any place of worship, or maintain any ministry, contrary to, or against, his own free will and consent: Nor can any man, who acknowledges the being of a God, be justly deprived or abridged of any civil right as a citizen, on account of his religious sentiments or peculiar mode of religious worship: And that no authority can or ought to be vested in, or assumed by any power whatever, that shall in any case interfere with, or in any manner control, the right of conscience in the free exercise of religious worship.
Pennsylvania, 1776

SECT. 2. That all men have a natural and unalienable right to worship Almighty God according to the dictates of their own consciences and understandings; and that no man ought or of right can be compelled to attend any religious worship or maintain any ministry contrary to or against his own free will and consent, and that no authority can or ought to be vested in, or assumed by any power whatever that shall in any case interfere with, or in any manner control the right of conscience in the free exercise of religious worship.

SECT. 3. That all persons professing the Christian religion ought forever to enjoy equal rights and privileges in this state, unless, under colour of religion, any man disturb the peace, the happiness or safety of society. Delaware, 1776

XXXIII. That, as it is the duty of every man to worship God in such manner as he thinks most acceptable to him; all persons, professing the Christian religion, are equally entitled to protection in their religious liberty; wherefore no person ought by any law to be molested in his person or estate on account of his religious persuasion or profession, or for his religious practice; unless, under colour of religion, any man shall disturb the good order, peace or safety of the State, or shall infringe the laws of morality, or injure others, in their natural, civil, or religious rights; nor ought any person to be compelled to frequent or maintain, or contribute, unless on contract, to maintain any particular place of worship or any particular ministry. Maryland, 1776

XIX. That all men have a natural and unalienable right to worship Almighty God according to the dictates of their own consciences. North Carolina, 1776

III. That all men have a natural and unalienable right to worship ALMIGHTY GOD, according to the dictates of their own consciences and understanding, regulated by the word of GOD; and that no man ought, or of right can be compelled to attend any religious worship, or erect, or support any place of worship, or maintain any minister, contrary to the dictates of his conscience; nor can any man who professes the protestant religion, be justly deprived or abridged of any civil right, as a citizen, on account of his religious sentiment, or peculiar mode of religious worship, and that no authority can, or ought to be vested in, or assumed by, any power whatsoever, that shall, in any case, interfere with, or in any manner control, the rights of conscience, in the free exercise of religious worship: nevertheless, every sect or denomination of people ought to observe the Sabbath, or the Lord's day, and keep up, and support, some sort of religious worship, which to them shall seem most agreeable to the revealed will of GOD. Vermont, 1777

II. It is the right as well as the duty of all men in society, publicly, and at stated seasons, to worship the SUPREME BEING, the great Creator and Preserver of the universe. And no subject shall be hurt, molested, or restrained, in his person, liberty, or estate, for worshipping GOD in the manner and season most agreeable to the dictates of his own conscience; or for his religious profession of sentiments; provided he doth not disturb the public peace, or obstruct others in their religious worship.
Massachusetts, 1780

IV. Among the natural rights, some are in their very nature unalienable, because no equivalent can be given or received for them. Of this kind are the RIGHTS OF CONSCIENCE.

V. Every individual has a natural and unalienable right to worship GOD according to the dictates of his own conscience, and reason; and no subject shall be hurt, molested, or restrained in his person, liberty or estate for worshipping GOD, in the manner and season most agreeable to the dictates of his own conscience, or for his religious profession, sentiments or persuasion; provided he doth not disturb the public peace, or disturb others, in their religious worship. New Hampshire, 1784[6]

As for the rest of the new states, New York, New Jersey, South Carolina, and Georgia made similar constitutional provisions.[7] The charters of Rhode Island and Connecticut, issued in 1662 and 1663 respectively, included provision for a guarantee of liberty of conscience as has been noted already.

The sections cited clearly show a devotion to liberty of conscience. An examination of these sections, however, from the perspective of the problem of authority shows more fully the relationship between the view of conscience expressed in the constitutions and that found in the tradition of William Perkins.

Earlier in this study it has been argued that the advocates of liberty of conscience in the seventeenth century were devoted to the belief that God alone is Lord of conscience.[8] God alone was Head of the church through Jesus Christ; God was the Chief Magistrate as well. The final authority in each sphere was God, for He was the Creator and sustainer of all things.

From the point of view of advocates of liberty of conscience, a further consideration was essential. Conscience was finally the normative factor in determining God's will, even as it affected the operation of the state and churches. Of course conscience was enlightened by the Bible and experience in general, but in the existential situation it was conscience that determined what it was that a man must do. The Westminster Confession phrased this view in a pithy fashion, as has been noted: "God alone is Lord of the conscience, and has set it free from the doctrines and commandments of men."[9] Further, it stated that to obey such doctrines and commandments in blind obedience was a betrayal of true liberty of conscience.[10] Obviously men must obey certain doctrines and commandments, but only when they were according to the will of God as determined by conscience.

This stance was termed a "theology of conscience" in an earlier chapter,[11] and that characterization requires further elaboration, since it continued to be a critical feature of the concept of conscience in the era of the American Revolution. In the twentieth century, when a "death of God" theology can be seriously promoted, when most academic intellectuals, and political ones for that matter, would be embarrassed by any reference to theology, mention of a theology of conscience has little meaning. The phenomenon that "theology of conscience" refers to, however, may be recognized under another label. *Religion* in its broad and historic sense comes close to being synonomous with the word *theology* as used until the twentieth century. In each case the word refers to how it is that man relates to his Creator, or how all aspects of reality evident in the creation relate to the Creator.

In the language of sphere sovereignty, conscience of man is normative in all spheres because it is precisely this feature of man, as creature, that God placed in a position superior to his other qualities. As was noted earlier, writers on the subject called conscience "the principle of our acting," "the wheel that must set all the rest going," "a thing out of men's jurisdiction," "the highest sovereignty under heaven." Further, conscience has "more force and power to work upon men, than all other agents"; as such "it will neither be beholden to man for its liberty, nor is it capable of his restraints, it is out of the reach of all human power."[12] With these characteristics in mind it is easier to appreciate the meaning of Robert Saunderson when he said, "There cannot be imagined a higher contempt of God than for a man to despise the power of his own conscience."[13] Clearly conscience in this view is considered normative for life and all conceivable aspects that it encompasses. If *religion* means the stance a person takes in relating the basic issues of life, to use the broadest conception, the phenomenon referred to as a "theology of conscience" is surely a definition of religion. It is this theology of conscience as a pervasive religious outlook which came to full fruition in American soil during the eighteenth century. The logical outgrowth of this religious view of life was manifest in the new constitutions, in the provisions for liberty of conscience, and in the general framework of such provisions.

Focusing on the section of the Virginia constitution cited above for a moment, it is evident that the intent was to link "Creator" "religion," and "conscience." Religion is the way that a man relates to his Creator, but this relationship can be cared for only through conscience. Conscience employs reason and conviction, not force and violence; hence, conscience as the only way to discharge the duties of man toward his Creator must be at liberty. Significantly, the Virginia constitution adds that it is necessary, therefore, to practice "Christian forbearance, love, and charity towards each other." This provision implies two important assumptions, first that the whole business of Creator-religion-conscience is in a Christian context, and that it involves not only a relationship between one man and his God, but also the relationship of each man to the next. Conscience is thus normative in the broadest sense of religion.[14]

The same characteristics are evident in the other state constitutions. Pennsylvania speaks positively of the right to worship "Almighty God" according to conscience. That religion was an inclusive term, meaning more than mere formal worship, is clear from the phrases "religious sentiments" and "peculiar mode of worship," they being viewed as distinguishable but complementary. As if conscious of the English practice of tolerating certain acts of conscience, the Pennsylvania constitution also stated that "no authority can or ought to be vested in, or assumed by any power whatever, that shall in any case interfere with ... the rights of conscience."[15] These same measures were stated in the Delaware document.[16] Maryland's provisions differed slightly, chiefly in that it used the word "religious liberty" in place of the word *conscience*.[17] North Carolina phrased liberty of conscience in a single sentence, using the same words that had appeared in several other states, namely, "That all men have a natural and unalienable right to worship Almighty God according to the dictates of their own consciences."[18] Vermont followed earlier measures, injecting the phrase "regulated by the word of GOD" as a qualification of the meaning of the word *conscience*.[19] Massachusetts combined the Virginia notion that religion was a duty with that of other states which viewed it as a right. The universal character of religion was, in Massachusetts, acknowledged through reference to God as the Supreme Being, the Creator and Preserver of the universe.[20]

From the perspective of the problem of authority, from the perspective of sphere sovereignty, it is evident from the foregoing that the state constitutional provisions for liberty of conscience were cast in the language and context that had been stated for generations by advocates of liberty of conscience in the tradition of William Perkins. When the new state constitutions at the time of the American Revolution spoke of liberty of conscience, they continued a longstanding tradition, elevating it to the level of a constitutional guarantee.

Looking at the Revolutionary period as a whole, it is important to appreciate the significance of these provisions in the states. They indicated the range and scope of interest and devotion to the idea of liberty of conscience. When Madison spoke of a great concern among Americans as to the fate of the rights of conscience under the new federal government, a point noted at the beginning of this chapter,[21] he was aware of the universal provision for liberty of conscience in the state constitutions. Recognition of the states' support and provision for liberty of conscience also provides some insight into certain portions of the Declaration of Independence, a subject on which attention may now be profitably focused.

B. *Liberty of Conscience and the Declaration of Independence*

Further light on the place of liberty of conscience in the era of the American Revolution may be gained by a careful examination of the Declaration of Independence. In turning to an examination of the Declaration, however, it needs to be pointed out that the Revolution has often been written about in terms of a conflict between the Declaration and the federal Constitution. This view suggests that the Declaration is the true symbol of the Revolution, while the Constitution represents a conservative counter-revolution.²² Such a view obscures the fundamental characteristics that these documents have in common; and it tends to detach them from the constitutions and declarations of the states.

Much can be learned from viewing all these documents as evidence of a general "climate of opinion," to borrow Carl Becker's famous phrase. From this perspective, the Declaration appeals as a brief statement of purpose and ideals, much like a church's creedal statement; thus it may be taken as a summary of more elaborate views. In light of the fact that the new states all provided for liberty of conscience, the question may be asked whether the Declaration said anything about the rights of conscience. This is a crucial question, since the text of the Declaration does not include the word *conscience*.

Staughton Lynd's provocative essay on the intellectual origins of American radicalism has as a central theme the notion that the Declaration assumes the rights of conscience as it argues for liberty.[23] Lynd focuses on the meaning of the phrase "unalienable right." Traditionally, says Lynd, this phrase has been interpreted by analogy to property rights, but "inalienability thus defined did not exclude the permanent transfer of a right from the original owner to a delegated purchaser."[24] The logic of the analogy to property rights leads to the conclusion that liberty, being one of the unalienable rights referred to in the Declaration, could also be transferred. Says Lynd, this "was the fatal flaw in the traditional theories of natural rights," that is, that an individual could give up his liberty as he could give up his property.[25]

Having demonstrated the poverty of reading the phrase "unalienable rights" by analogy to property rights, Lynd suggests that the correct way to understand this phrase is by "analogy to conscience."[26] Quoting a mid-eighteenth-century writer on moral philosophy, Lynd states that the rights of conscience are unalienable because they cannot be subject to the will of another, the nature of conscience requiring this characteristic. Summing up, he says, "When rights were 'unalienable' in this sense, it did not mean that they could not be transferred without consent [property view], but that their nature made them untransferable [conscience]."[27]

Lynd recognized that his interpretation was a substantial departure from the traditional view. The problem with the "Becker-Bailyn" thesis is that it looked only at the "bare surface" of the language, says Lynd, ignoring the context in which it appeared.[28] What needed clarification was the "intellectual background," says Lynd, and the background in Lynd's view was "largely in England." The key figures were a group of radicals, "associated with non-Anglican (Nonconformist or Dissenting) Protestant denominations such as the Quakers."[29] Their significance rests in the fact that they "transferred to secular political discourse that reliance on the individual conscience of uneducated men for which they had contended in religion."[30] These Radicals, as Lynd styles them, therein affirmed what they like to call " 'the dignity of human nature.' "[31] This secularization of the concept of conscience took place in the 1770's, according to Lynd.

Lynd is undoubtedly correct in seeing the significance of the concept of conscience in the milieu of the Declaration of Independence. He presents a persuasive argument for its appearance among his Radicals in the 1770's, but the purpose of his study has precluded his seeing an even greater influence of the idea at the time of the Revolution. Lynd's mission in his essay was to find respectable roots for the views he and his associates hold in the twentieth century, though he does not say this in explicit terms.[32] The significance of conscience for him was that it "internalized" and "humanized" the standard for rights.[33] If he is correct in pointing to an internal standard for rights, then his contemporaries who lean so heavily on property rights are not in the true American tradition.

Lynd's characterization of his Radicals cannot be avoided, but the question remains as to how the rest of society viewed the rights of conscience. In looking at the Declaration only for the moment, it appears that another dimension of the concept of conscience was as important as the notion that "their nature [rights of conscience] made them untransferable."[34] The question of authority is crucial in any view of conscience; in fact, the claim of conscience is no better than the authority called upon. Lynd says that his Radicals "secularized" and "humanized" the concept of conscience,[35] and this would seem to require an appeal to "human rights" as authority in the Declaration. While many men in the twentieth century might gain an audience by appealing to "human rights" as they call for liberty of conscience, such a view would have been unintelligible to most men of the eighteenth century. The framers of the Declaration thus reached for the best argument from authority which they knew, one which their audience understood well. "Men . . . are endowed by their Creator with certain unalienable rights," they said, and to them this was a self-evident truth.[36] In other words, certain rights, like the rights of conscience, cannot be alienated, *not* because they are "human rights," rather because they are an endowment from their Creator.

The question of authority in the Declaration's claim that certain rights were unalienable is most important, for related to it is the question of what limits, if any, there are on liberty. If Lynd is correct in seeing "unalienable rights" as an expression of "human rights," then the limits depend upon what one person sees, or a group agrees to, as the limit of liberty. This could lead to totalitarianism if the "people" agreed to that stance through acquiescence or by design. On the other hand, it could lead to an exaggerated degree of individual liberty, even to anarchy, if a sufficient number of the American public agreed that conscience allowed this degree of liberty. Revolution would be an absolute right for each person if he was persuaded in his conscience that revolution was the answer to his particular problem. Jefferson and others recognized revolution as a right, but in that view it depended upon a substantial segment of the community agreeing to that course of action. Lynd laments the fact that revolution could occur only when a "majority" of the people favored it; to him that seemed unfair and unworkable.[37] The only way to avoid totalitarianism and anarchy, and to avoid Lynd's conclusion concerning revolution, is to appreciate the argument from authority used in the Declaration. That argument is the same one noted earlier in the state constitutions, namely, the argument for conscience and its liberty in the context of sphere sovereignty.

From the perspective of sphere sovereignty it appears that the Declaration of Independence was as much of a comment on liberty of conscience as were the state constitutions. Staughton Lynd's perceptive analysis of the Declaration shows that the phrase "unalienable rights" can make sense only in terms of a concept of conscience as the basis for this phrase. While he failed to appreciate the broad support for the idea in the period, his conclusion as to the significance of conscience for the meaning of the Declaration is a substantial contribution toward a better understanding of the Declaration. Lynd's focusing on the phrase "unalienable rights" as a crucial feature is supported by the fact that the state constitutions also used the same phrase when speaking of conscience and its rights. Further, the argument from authority, the source of authority appealed to in the Declaration, was the same one employed in the state constitutions. In sum, then, concerning the Declaration of Independence, it may be concluded liberty of conscience was an ideal, and at the same time an assumption implicit in the document.

C. *Liberty of Conscience and the Federal Constitution*

Since the Revolution also brought forth a new Federal Constitution, it is important to inquire what provision it contained for the rights of conscience. The emergence of the Federal Constitution in 1787 created a crisis in the minds of many concerning the protection of their rights, rights which were protected in the states. The story is well known how the ratification of the Constitution involved heated debates by its admirers and detractors, and how the question of protection of rights was a central issue.[38] In fact, two states refused to ratify the Constitution at all until some such provision was made.[39] Still others ratified it on the condition that protection of rights would be established immediately.[40]

As the first Congress met in 1789, therefore, one of the first items presented for the agenda was consideration of a way to protect the rights of citizens. There were differences of opinion among the membership as to the import of this issue. Some argued that the people expected them to get on with creating the government that the Constitution envisioned,[41] but others argued that the Constitution was, in fact, incomplete without specific provisions for the rights of the people.[42] One argument pointed out that the Preamble to the Constitution stated, among other things, that it was ordained to "secure the blessings of liberty," and that this was the only item in the list of stated purposes that had not been provided for in the text of the document. For this reason, the document was incomplete.

The great majority of the House agreed that something had to be done about the question of rights, but it was James Madison who took it upon himself to assemble a list of the items that the state conventions and others deemed essential to "secure the blessings of liberty." As he said, "I shall proceed to bring the amendments befor you . . . and advocate them until they shall be finally adopted or rejected by a Constitutional majority of this House."[43] His original list included some twenty propositions aimed at a variety of grievances.[44] When the smoke cleared and Congress was ready to propose amendments to the states, twelve remained, ten of which passed into the Constitution.[45]

The ten amendments to the Constitution were all part of a single item in Madison's original list;[46] obviously, therefore, his original proposals were stated in greater detail. The abbreviation, however, of them is an important clue to an understanding of the intent of each amendment. What turned out to be the First Amendment in the Constitution was stated in the following manner by Madison:

> The civil rights of none shall be abridged on account of religious belief or worship, nor shall any national religion be established, nor shall the full and equal rights of conscience be in any manner, or on any pretext, infringed.
>
> The people shall not be deprived or abridged of their right to speak, to write, or to publish their sentiments; and the freedom of press, as one of the great bulwarks of liberty, shall be inviolable.
>
> The people shall not be restrained from peaceably assembling and consulting for their common good; nor from applying to the legislature by petition, or remonstrances, for redress of their grievances.[47]

Obviously the first paragraph above was shortened to the familiar phrase, "Congress shall make no law respecting an establishment of religion, or prohibiting the free exercise thereof. . . ." Equally obvious is the fact that Madison's proposal concerning "religion" and the federal government assumed a relationship between conscience and religion.

Further light on what this relationship was may be found in other parts of the House debates on amendments, particularly in two other proposals by Madison, and in comments on them. In the proposed amendment concerning the right to keep and bear arms, Madison included a phrase aimed at preventing the abuse of the rights of conscience in the case of those who objected to bearing arms. After some discussion it was decided that conscientious objection to bearing arms was not a right in the fundamental sense, because it could create a situation in which no one would bear arms, even if the national safety depended upon it. In terms of sphere sovereignty, this was a situation in which the limits of the liberty due man was determined by the legitimate needs of the state as it pursued its stated purpose. In other words, liberty of conscience was limited by the inherent rights and duties of the sphere called *state*. The House members were sure that the government would be sympathetic to the desires of conscientious objectors, but they made it clear that objection to bearing arms was not a right of conscience. Fear that no one would want to bear arms was not based upon a distrust of Quakers or Mennonites; rather, such fear was based upon the belief that some day non-Christians, people without a Christian conception of conscience, would use such a provision as shelter.[48]

Madison also proposed an amendment protecting liberty of conscience in the states. It read, "No State shall violate the equal rights of conscience."[49] In debate it was argued that this was out of place, because the federal government had no authority to alter the state constitutions; such an amendment surely would be such an alteration. Madison, however, conceived this to be the most important amendment in the whole list, his reason being, "If there were any reason to restrain the Government of the United States from infringing upon these essential rights, it was equally necessary that they should be secured against State Governments."[50] It was at this point that Madison gave the argument cited in the beginning of this chapter, namely, that protection for liberty of conscience was absolutely vital, since it was unprotected in the British constitution.[51]

Viewed together, Madison's three proposals touching on the subject of conscience present a consistent picture of the place of conscience in the definition of *religion,* but the comments of other House members are enlightening, also. Of particular interest was the discussion on the proposed wording, namely, "no religion shall be established by law, nor shall the equal rights of conscience be infringed," this being offered as a substitute for the longer version.[52] One member suggested that the clauses of the sentence be transposed, so as to preclude it being read as a discouragement to religion.[53] Next it was suggested that the first clause should read "no religious doctrine shall be established by law."[54] Still another thought that the whole amendment should be eliminated, because the only issue was that concerning "religious establishments," and that the Constitution had not delegated any authority whatsoever in this area to Congress.[55] Further, Representative Carroll indicated why he thought the amendment should stand:

> As the rights of conscience are, in their nature, of peculiar delicacy, and will little bear the gentlest touch of governmental hand; and as many sects have concurred in opinion that they are not well secured under the present Constitution . . . (I am) much in favor of adopting the words.[56]

Carroll was sure that this amendment would quiet the public more than any other amendment he had heard proposed. Significantly, he added that "he would not contend with gentlemen about the phraseology" because his object was to secure the substance in such a "manner as to satisfy the wishes of the honest part of the community."[57]

Madison again joined the debate and said that he thought the meaning of the words to be "that Congress should not establish a religion, and enforce the legal observation of it by law, nor to compel men to worship God in any manner contrary to their conscience."[58] Whether the words were necessary or not, Madison said he did not know, but he was certain "that they had been required by some of the State Conventions" because they believed that the Constitution gave the government power to make all laws necessary to carry on the government. The conventions saw this as power to "make laws of such a nature as might infringe the rights of conscience, and establish a national religion." To quiet this fear on the part of the conventions and others was the purpose of the amendment, said Madison.[59]

Another aspect of the subject was pointed out by Representative Huntington; he "feared, with the gentleman first up on this subject, that the words might be taken in such latitude as to be extremely hurtful to the cause of religion."[60] He understood it in the sense stated by Madison, he said, but others might put another construction on it. Huntington illustrated his point with an example. He noted that some congregations supported their ministers and built their church buildings by contributions, contrasting this with taxing for this purpose as occurred in some places. Agreements to contribute for these purposes were written into church by-laws, he said, placing a contractual obligation upon the contributor. Suppose, he said, that an action were brought before a federal court upon failure of performance in such a case. Huntington was fearful that the "no establishment" clause might be interpreted to mean that the defaulting person could not be compelled to performance of his obligation. In conclusion, Huntington said that he hoped the amendment "would be made in such a way as to secure the rights of conscience . . . but not to patronise those who professed no religion at all."[61]

The result of these discussions was the adoption of the statement, "Congress shall make no law establishing religion, or to prevent the free exercise thereof, or to infringe the rights of conscience."[62] Subsequently, the House's proposed amendment went to the Senate, and finally, to the Committee of Conference. The record of the House and Senate does not show at what point the above version was changed to read, "Congress shall make no law respecting an establishment of religion, or prohibiting the free exercise thereof," this being the form finally ratified by the states.[63]

Obviously the final form submitted to the states did not include the word *conscience*, and the records of the Senate and Committee of Conference do not indicate why specific reference to conscience was not made, that is, why the version submitted to the states was altered. At first glance it would appear that this change was of major importance, but reflection upon the context of the debates and upon the character of the climate of opinion at the time of the Revolution suggests that the change was very minor. If the omission of the clause on conscience was of major importance, if it altered radically the intent of the House in its earlier draft, then it might be expected that, as the final form came to the House, those who vigorously supported the cause of conscience would have objected to the omission. No objections were raised.[64] The omission of specific reference to conscience in the final form may be readily understood, however, by reference to the general climate of opinion of the era. Noted earlier was the fact that the framers of the state constitutions assumed that religion was inseparable from conscience and its rights. From this perspective it would make sense to shorten the proposed amendment through eliminating redundancies. In other words, "free exercise of religion" and "the rights of conscience" referred to the same thing; nothing was lost through striking out one of these two phrases.

To summarize and emphasize the development of the place of conscience in the First Amendment, the main versions of it in the House debates may be cited again:

> The civil rights of none shall be abridged on account of religious belief or worship, nor shall any national religion be established, nor shall the full and equal rights of conscience be in any manner, or on any pretext, infringed. June 8, 1789

> No religion shall be established by law, nor shall the equal rights of conscience be infringed. August 15, 1789

> Congress shall make no law establishing religion, or to prevent the free exercise thereof, or to infringe the rights of conscience. August 20, 1789

> Congress shall make no law respecting an establishment of religion, or prohibiting the free exercise thereof. September 25, 1789[65]

The absence of the clause containing the word *conscience* in the version submitted to the states on September 25, 1789, may be understood when the word *religion* is recognized as another way to refer to conscience and its rights.

Having examined the state constitutions, the Declaration of Independence, and the background of the First Amendment in light of the history of the claim of liberty of conscience, it appears that concern for the rights of conscience at the time of the Revolution was based upon the belief that conscience was central in man's life. Further, this view of conscience, rooted in the conception of conscience that emerged in the seventeenth century, was the prevailing one at the time of the American Revolution, since universal provision for it was made in the new instruments of government created during the Revolution. The pervasive character of this view is also evident in the fact that it appeared in the context of sphere sovereignty, specifically in the provision that no authority or power could or ought to be vested in anyone so as to interfere with the rights of conscience.

Notwithstanding these conclusions, one further question deserves consideration, that is, how was it that provision could be made for liberty of conscience and at the same time provision made in some states for the support of public worship. This is an important consideration, because historians often point out a disparity between states on this subject,[66] and because it will help toward a better understanding of the First Amendment.

Much is made of the fact, for example, that Massachusetts is said to have had a state church until the 1830's, this being contrasted with the Virginia provision for "dis-establishment" during the Revolution.[67] The conclusion is usually drawn that Virginia was somehow more enlightened than Massachusetts. A careful reading of the Massachusetts Constitution in light of the concept of conscience set forth in this study helps toward a better understanding of this unique situation. Article I stated that all men have certain "natural essential, and unalienable rights," a statement found in many of the other constitutions.[68] Article II provided for liberty of conscience in the following form:

> II. It is the right as well as the duty of all men in society, publicly, and at stated seasons, to worship the SUPREME BEING, the great Creator and Preserver of the universe. And no subject shall be hurt, molested, or restrained, in his person, liberty, or estate, for worshipping GOD in the manner and season most

agreeable to the dictates of his own conscience; or for his religious profession of sentiments; provided he doth not disturb the public peace, or obstruct others in their religious worship.[69]

Like Article I, this article differs little from that of other states. The notion that Massachusetts somehow provided for "an establishment" of religion hinges upon the meaning of Article III.[70] It had several sections, the first of which gave authority to the legislature to encourage "public worship" because "the happiness of a people, and the good order and preservation of civil government" depend upon religion. Further, it gave political and religious societies power to arrange for the support of public worship, and it suggested that citizens be enjoined to attend public worship. There was no doubt about the fact that this meant that taxes could be imposed for the support of public worship. Without reference to the rest of the article, this arrangement could be called "an establishment" of religion.

But Article III has more to say. Crucial to the intent of the above provision for public support was the next phrase, "if there be any on whose instructions they can *conscientiously* and conveniently attend."[71] In other words, the provisions could not violate the previously stated rights of conscience. Further comment on the provision in question appeared in the next phrase, which said that all political and religious societies shall at all times have "the exclusive right of electing" and supporting their teachers. As for the money, it was to be used for the support of whatever "religious sect or denomination" one chose. Finally, Article III stated that every denomination "shall be equally under the protection of the law" and that "no subordination of any one sect or denomination to another shall ever be established by law."[72]

The last sections make it amply clear that the writers of the Constitution did not intend "an establishment" of religion in Massachusetts. No one denomination was to be exclusively enthroned as the official church of the state, as in the case of England, for example. The question remains, however, as to the meaning of the earlier provisions of Article III. Encouraging people to attend public worship and giving authority to the legislature to provide support for such worship certainly appears to be state establishment of church. It is precisely at this point that the concept of conscience as outlined in this essay aids in understanding.

There is no conflict between Article II's provision for liberty of conscience and Article III's provision for the support of public worship, when liberty of conscience means liberty to do one's religion, or the duty he owes his Creator. Article II in fact stated, "It is the right as well as the duty of all men in society . . . to worship the Supreme Being, the great Creator and Preserver of the universe"; therefore, "no subject shall be hurt, molested, or restrained . . . for worshipping God in the manner and season most agreeable to the dictates of his own conscience."[73] This provision could be made alongside of one that talked of support for public worship, when the latter is recognized as *encouragement* of public worship, rather than "an establishment" in the sense of a state church.

The issue concerning the stance of a state toward "religion" needs to be understood well. The Massachusetts constitution's provisions make sense only when the word *religion* is understood in the sense that prevailed in the eighteenth century, namely, as an all-inclusive view of life. This is what the writers of the Massachusetts constitution had in mind when they stated that the happiness of a people and the success of a government depended upon religion.[74] Conscience was the normative factor in religion, and so it had to be free from all interference. From this perspective, encouragement of religion was natural and inevitable. Clearly, however, liberty of conscience and encouragement of religion were very different from the question of an established form of religion, the latter being expressly prohibited in Massachusetts as it was in most, if not all, other states. As for the change in the Massachusetts constitution in the 1830's concerning religion, it testifies to a sustained desire on the part of that state's citizens to encourage religion, not a continuation of a state church, as has so often been argued.

The distinction between encouragement of religion and establishment of it found in the Massachusetts constitution provides a further insight into the meaning of the First Amendment to the federal Constitution. Noted earlier was the fact that during the process of drafting the First Amendment *religion* was viewed as being protected through liberty of conscience.[75] This feature, together with the distinction made concerning the Massachusetts constitution, provides the basis for a full appreciation of the First Amendment.

The familiar form of the First Amendment, finally ratified by the states in 1791, had three main ideas.[76] The first is clear enough, "Congress shall make no law." The second, "respecting an establishment of religion," has caused some difficulty and confusion among constitutional lawyers. In view of the Massachusetts constitution's provision, "no subordination of any one sect or denomination to another shall ever be established by law,"[77] it appears that this statement could mean only one thing, that Congress shall make no law respecting a religious establishment, that it shall make no law elevating or subordinating any sect or denomination; in other words, that it shall not create a national religious establishment, or church. This view is fully consistent with the debates in the House noted earlier, debates on precisely this point. The third idea, "or prohibiting the free exercise thereof," has also caused some difficulty for constitutional lawyers. As in the case of the second idea on establishments, this one depends upon the statement, "Congress shall make no law." In addition, the intent of the words, "or prohibiting the free exercise thereof," refer back to the phrase, "respecting an establishment of religion." *Religion* is the key word in each case; hence, the meaning of the third idea is that Congress shall make no law prohibiting the free exercise of religion. Translated into the language of conscience, this phrase would read, Congress shall make no law prohibiting the free exercise of conscience. The equation of *religion* and *conscience* is as crucial as it is legitimate, for it is only then that the First Amendment provides a framework within which actions can be judged by a commonly accepted standard.

The First Amendment, like the Massachusetts constitution, prevented governmental interference in the area of establishments or churches. In view of the fact that the states encouraged religion, the question arises whether the First Amendment also encouraged religion. Whether the phrase, "or prohibiting the free exercise thereof," is read with or without reference to the equation of "religion" and "conscience," it seems obvious that the restriction on Congress is an encouragement of religion. The difference between Massachusetts' strong encouragement and the First Amendment's mild provision does not alter the basic stance, for in each case the standard finally rests on the operation of conscience.

Appreciation of the place of conscience in the formulation of the First Amendment requires some adjustments in the currently accepted attitudes toward the amendment, particularly in the case of the separationist doctrine. Borrowing from a view stated by Thomas Jefferson in a letter to the Danbury Baptists' Association, written a decade after the First Amendment was ratified, the separationist doctrine talks about "a wall of separation."[78] Often the phrase is used in the argument to eliminate prayers in Congress and the motto, "In God we trust," from coins. When used this way, it is clear that the phrase intends a wall of separation between the state and religion, though at times the word *church* is used when religion is intended.

The separationist doctrine is based upon two erroneous assumptions, one touching the intent of Jefferson's phrase, and the other touching the amendment's use of the word *religion*. Jefferson did not intend to imply a "wall of separation" between religion and the state when *religion* is understood to mean any expressions or actions that refer to God, such as the prayers in Congress or the motto on coins. Jefferson's letter stated:

> Believing with you that religion is a matter which lies solely between man and his God, that he owes account to none other for his faith or his worship, that the legislative powers of government reach *actions only*, and not opinions, I contemplate with sovereign reverence that act of the whole American people which declared that their legislature should "make no law respecting an establishment of religion, or prohibiting the free exercise thereof," thus building a wall of separation between *church* and state.[79]

Clearly he believed that the First Amendment placed a wall of separation between church and state, but he uses the word *church* in a different way than he uses the word *religion* in this letter. *Church* refers to "an establishment" of religion, and in this he is consistent with his contemporaries' use of the word. *Religion* in the first part is the same concept used by others at that time; it is the matter which lies between man and God, and it is beyond the reach of others, whether a matter of faith or worship. Jefferson's use of the word *religion* in this letter makes even more sense if it is read with an eye to the place of conscience in the whole affair. In his *Notes on Virginia* Jefferson demonstrated that he assumed conscience was normative in religion. Speaking of religion he said, "Our rulers can have no authority over such," because "the rights of conscience we never submitted, we could not submit."[80]

When the "wall of separation" is understood as Jefferson used it, to describe the relationship between the government and religious churches, it is obvious that the separationist view of religion is different from that used in the formulation of the First Amendment. As has been demonstrated, the framers of the amendment distinguished between organized religion, or church, and the free exercise of religion through conscience. If the men of Congress agree for reasons of conscience that they desire to pray before they commence their business, that would seem to be their privilege in view of the fact that the First Amendment prohibits interference with the free exercise of religion through conscience. The idea of a "wall of separation" has nothing to do with the free exercise of religion through conscience, either in Jefferson's letter, or in the context in which the First Amendment was formulated. Contrary to the separationist doctrine, the First Amendment saw religion as a phenomenon that could not be circumscribed in any manner, and this was true because conscience was the normative factor.

Advocates of the separationist doctrine also point to the comments of Jefferson and Madison on the question of the President proclaiming a national Day of Thanksgiving as evidence of the idea of a wall of separation.[81] Madison, after retirement from the presidency, stated that he did not think that it was a good practice, implying that it tended to violate the establishment provision of the First Amendment. Jefferson's position was the same.[82] If such proclamations required people to worship publicly, or to perform any act upon pain of penalty, then it could be concluded that the free exercise of religion had been interfered with. Proclamations do not require any performance, much less upon pain of penalty; rather, they encourage people to care for their religion through conscience. This encouragement comes from the desire and free choice of the man who is President, undoubtedly as an act of conscience. He is not required to make such a proclamation; he may choose to not issue such a proclamation, as Jefferson decided to do. The views of Jefferson and of Madison in this case are not normative of the meaning of the First Amendment; they are reactions of individual persons to the amendment.

In sum, then, concerning the notion that the First Amendment intended to establish a "wall of separation," it must be concluded that such a phrase could only refer to the intent of the first part of the amendment, namely, "Congress shall make no law respecting an establishment of religion," understanding "an establishment" to mean a national religious establishment or national church. The second provision, preventing the free exercise of religion, is thus left free to carry the intent Congress had in mind when it formulated the amendment, namely, that everyone, including the President, was free to exercise his religion through conscience. It would be better, however, to refrain from using the notion of a wall of separation altogether, especially since the phrase does not appear in the amendment, using instead the classic phrase, "an establishment" of religion. The virtue of this phrase lies in the fact that it serves to remind citizens of the long struggle waged against established churches. Moreover, it leaves the next phrase of the amendment unencumbered, allowing it to serve as an additional reminder that the free exercise of religion through conscience is a peculiarly American right; as Madison said, "one unguarded in the British Constitution."

In conclusion, concerning liberty of conscience in the eighteenth century, the era of the American Revolution was most important. It was the time when a fundamental reordering of American society occurred, an occasion in which liberty of conscience was established in all states and in the new federal Constitution. The pervasive provision for liberty of conscience during the American Revolution was made because the public in general, and constitution writers in particular, regarded liberty of conscience as normative for man in caring for religion, and by religion they meant the comprehensive manner in which man relates to all reality. Recognition of conscience as normative in this way also carried a commitment to the idea of sphere sovereignty, that is, that various aspects of life are unique and limited to specific purposes. Most obvious examples of such spheres were those of government and organized religion. As the Revolution came to full fruition with the creation of the federal Constitution, the commitment to liberty of conscience was embodied in the structure of the central government through the First Amendment. This amendment prevented Congress from creating a national religious establishment, or church, and it guaranteed the free exercise of religion as broadly defined, through conscience.

The First Amendment is thus a great watershed in the history of the struggle for liberty of conscience, for it was the culmination of a long battle for the recognition of that idea set forth among Cambridge Puritans and advanced by an ever-increasing number of people during the seventeenth and eighteenth centuries. At the same time, the First Amendment laid the foundation for an unprecedented degree of freedom through conscience.

CHAPTER NOTES

1. Joseph Gales, comp., *The Debates and Proceedings in the Congress of the United States* (Washington, 1834), I, p. 766; hereinafter cited as Gales, *Debates*.
2. *Ibid.*, p. 436.
3. *Ibid.*
4. *Journals of the Continental Congress, 1774-1789* (Washington, 1906), IV, p. 3.
5. *Supra*, p. 129 ff.
6. Francis N. Thorpe, ed., *The Federal and State Constitutions, Colonial Charters, and Other Organic Laws* (Washington, 1909); hereinafter cited as Thorpe, *Constitutions*. The sections cited may be found as follows: Va., VII, pp. 3812-3824; Pa., V, pp. 3081-3084; Del., II, p. 695 ff.; Md., III, pp. 1686-1691; N. C., V, pp. 2787-2789; Vt., VI, pp. 3434-3442; Mass., III, pp. 1888-1893; and N. H., IV, pp. 2453-2457.
7. *Ibid.*, N. Y., V, p. 2637; N. J., V, p. 2567; S. C., V, p. 2757; and Ga., II, p. 773.
8. *Supra*, p. 86 ff.

9. *Supra*, p. 86.
10. *Ibid.*
11. *Supra*, p. 16 ff.
12. *Supra*, pp. 92-93.
13. *Supra*, p. 92.
14. Thorpe, *Constitutions*, VII, pp. 3812-3824.
15. *Ibid.*, V, p. 3081.
16. *Ibid.*, pp. 695 ff.
17. *Ibid.*, III, p. 1686.
18. *Ibid.*, V, p. 2787.
19. *Ibid.*, VI, p. 3437.
20. *Ibid.*, III, p. 1888.
21. *Supra*, p. 157.
22. A convenient summary may be found in R. A. Billington, ed., *The Reinterpretation of Early American History* (San Marino, 1966), p. 101 ff., written by Merril Jensen. Jensen's work is a prime example of the view commented on in the text, and thus should be read in conjunction with Robert Brown's *Charles Beard and the Constitution* (New York, 1965).
23. Staughton Lynd, *The Intellectual Origins of American Radicalism* (New York, 1969), hereinafter cited as Lynd, *Radicalism*.
24. *Ibid.*, p. 45.
25. *Ibid.*
26. *Ibid.*
27. *Ibid.*, p. 45.
28. *Ibid.*, p. 19.
29. *Ibid.*
30. *Ibid.*
31. *Ibid.*, p. 20.
32. *Ibid.*, p. 3 ff.
33. *Ibid.*, p. 19 ff.
34. *Ibid.*, p. 45.
35. *Ibid.*, p. 19 ff.
36. *The Constitution of the United States of America and the Declaration of Independence* (New York), published by Doubleday and Co., Inc., as a "New, Revised Edition," but without the name of the editor.
37. Lynd, *Radicalism*, p. 55.
38. Alfred H. Kelly and W. A. Harbison, *The American Constitution* (New York, 1963), pp. 148-160.
39. *Ibid.*
40. *Ibid.*
41. *Ibid.*, p. 434 ff.
42. *Ibid.*
43. Gales, *Debates*, p. 424.

44. *Ibid.*, pp. 433-436.
45. Alfred H. Kelly and W. A. Harbison, *The American Constitution* (New York, 1963), p. 176.
46. Gales, *Debates*, pp. 434-435.
47. *Ibid.*
48. *Ibid.*, p. 749.
49. *Ibid.*, p. 739; approved by House, p. 755.
50. *Ibid.*
51. *Ibid.*
52. *Ibid.*, p. 729.
53. *Ibid.*
54. *Ibid.*, p. 730.
55. *Ibid.*
56. *Ibid.*
57. *Ibid.*
58. *Ibid.*
59. *Ibid.*
60. *Ibid.*, pp. 730-731.
61. *Ibid.*
62. *Ibid.*, p. 766.
63. *Constitution and Declaration*, Doubleday edition.
64. Gales, *Debates*, pp. 434, 729, 766, and *Ibid.*, p. 47.
65. *Ibid.*
66. Every text examined covering either the Revolution or the period up to the 1830's follows the notion that a provision like that of Massachusetts, to be examined below, was an "establishment" or state church. See Kelly and Harbison, *The American Constitution*, cited above.
67. *Ibid.*
68. Thorpe, *Constitutions*, III, p. 1888.
69. *Ibid.*
70. *Ibid.*
71. *Ibid.* (italics mine).
72. *Ibid.*   73. *Ibid.*   74. *Ibid.*
75. *Supra*, p. 168 ff.
76. *Constitution and Declaration*, Doubleday edition.
77. Thorpe, *Constitutions*, III, p. 1888.
78. Leo Pfeffer, *Church State and Freedom*, "Introduction."
79. Saul K. Padover, *The Complete Jefferson* (New York, 1943), pp. 518-519 (italics mine).
80. Quoted in Joseph L. Blau, *Cornerstones of Religious Freedom in America* (Boston, 1949), p. 79.
81. Leo Pfeffer, *Church State and Freedom*, pp. 117-118.
82. *Ibid.*

Chapter VIII

CONCLUSION

In a broad perspective, it may be concluded that the guarantee of liberty of conscience at the time of the American Revolution, a guarantee set forth in the newly formed state constitutions and the First Amendment, was the result of a struggle that had roots deep in the past.

That conscience was at liberty in relation to other men and institutions was set forth in detail by the Elizabethan Puritan theologian William Perkins. With his declaration that Christ, in the New Testament, has given a liberty to conscience, he set out to indicate what this declaration meant for his contemporaries. To say that conscience was at liberty, and to say as he did that it was subject to God alone, was to say that it was sovereign in relation to other men and institutions. If conscience was sovereign, if conscience was at liberty, the jurisdiction that pertained to institutions such as the state was limited, distinct, and separate from other institutions. Perkins' view of conscience as sovereign and at liberty in relation to other men and institutions contrasted sharply, even radically, with that of English governmental officials. The governmental attitude toward conscience assumed that it came within the purview of the authority of the state, or its agent, the church. Matters of conscience, for them, were viewed as the object of a policy of toleration.

The difference in attitudes toward conscience evident in the age of Elizabeth became more pronounced during the era of the early Stuarts. Sectarian splinters of the Cambridge Puritan movement grasped the significance of the idea of conscience and its liberty for their belief that individuals were free under the New Testament to decide how and where they should perform their religious duties.

CONCLUSION

At the same time the governments of James I and Charles I continued to foster the idea that conscience came within the jurisdiction of governmental authority. As in the case of Elizabeth before them, certain actions based upon conscience might be tolerated, but the decision as to what fell within this policy of toleration, they believed, remained in the hands of governmental officials.

During the early years of the Stuart era, William Ames, a sometime student in Cambridge, created a system of theology which had as its normative principle the dialectic method of Peter Ramus. When Ames applied the dialectic method to the question of conscience, he locked conscience and its problems to the dialectic method, precluding the need or possibility of thinking of conscience in terms of liberty and sovereignty. When Ames's view of conscience was applied in practice in the Massachusetts Bay Colony, it precipitated a policy of toleration toward conscientious thoughts and actions. This was evident in the disputes which Massachusetts Bay leaders had with Roger Williams and Anne Hutchinson. Massachusetts Bay Colony thus, under its early leaders, had the same attitude toward conscience as did English government officials, though their position was based upon the systematic rationale of William Ames.

As the era of Civil War approached, liberty of conscience had become a familiar idea among a wide range of people. In the war era itself, liberty of conscience and sphere sovereignty were defended by the Divines of the Westminster Assembly, individually and collectively in the assembly's Confession of Faith. Levellers, supporters of Cromwell, as well as John Milton, Cromwell himself, and others, advocated liberty of conscience in the tradition of William Perkins.

As the Restoration began, many men in Old England continued to defend the claim of liberty of conscience, but the older concept of conscience as an object of governmental authority and power again came to dominate English society. The conflict between the idea of toleration and the idea of liberty concerning conscience came to an end in 1689 as the Act of Toleration was passed. This Act enshrined the long-held notion that conscience came within the purview of governmental authority, this remaining as official policy until the nineteenth century.

While liberty and sovereignty of conscience failed in Old England, it flourished in America from the earliest days of the colonial period. In addition to persistent individual defenses of liberty of conscience, as in the case of Roger Williams, liberty of conscience was provided for in most of the seventeenth-century charters, Massachusetts Bay Colony being the outstanding exception. By the end of the seventeenth century it became clear that liberty of conscience and its parallel idea of sphere sovereignty were emerging as important elements in the formation of an American political ideology. During the years after 1689, when John Locke published an important defense of liberty and sovereignty, colonial Americans increasingly drew upon his writings and those of other defenders of the idea, such as the Westminster Divines, to defend the claim of individual liberty. Liberty of conscience also was used in this period to argue for the separation of institutional spheres of jurisdiction.

As the Revolution came, Americans had expressed their devotion to liberty of conscience and sphere sovereignty in a variety of ways, in early charters, in individual pleas, and in their emerging political ideology. During the Revolution itself liberty of conscience was guaranteed as the new states were formed. Each state, in writing a new constitution, provided for liberty of conscience; the same guarantee appeared in the First Amendment. Sphere sovereignty as an integral feature of the idea of liberty of conscience was a useful tool at the time of the Revolution also, for it supported the belief of many that government was a separate, distinct, and limited institution. Liberty of conscience thus became a fundamental idea in the American mind.

Liberty of conscience had its roots deep in the past, in the works of the Puritan, William Perkins. Its history to the era of the American Revolution, and beyond, is the history of a Puritan idea.

BIBLIOGRAPHY

Adams. Thomas. *Works.* London, 1629.
American Weekly Mercury. Philadelphia, January, 1739/40.
Ames, William. *Conscience: Its Law or Cases, Five Books.* London, 1643.
―――. *Marrow of Theology.* J. D. Eusden, ed. Boston, 1968.
Andrews, C. M. *The Colonial Period of American History.* 4 vols. New Haven, 1964.
Ashley, Maurice. *Great Britain to 1688.* Ann Arbor, 1961.
Bailyn, Bernard. *The Ideological Origins of the American Revolution.* Cambridge, 1967.
Baker Book House. *The New Schaff-Herzog Encyclopedia of Religious Knowledge.* 13 vols. Grand Rapids, 1950.
Becker, Carl. *The Declaration of Independence.* New York, 1922.
―――. *The Heavenly City of the Eighteenth-Century Philosophers.* New Haven, 1932.
Bercovitch, Sacvan. "Typology in Puritan New England: The Williams-Cotton Controversy Reassessed," *American Quarterly,* XIX (Summer, 1967), pp. 166-191.
Bernard, Richard. *Christian Advertisements and Councils of Peace.* London, 1608.
Bigelow, J. *Molinos the Quietist.* New York, 1882.
Billington, R. A. (ed.). *The Reinterpretation of Early American History.* San Marino, 1966.
Blau, Joseph L. *Cornerstones of Religious Fredom in America.* Boston, 1949.
Bolam, George, *et al. The English Presbyterians.* Boston, 1968.
Bolles, John. *To Worship God in Spirit and in Truth, Is to Worship Him in True Liberty of Conscience.* Boston, 1756.
Brockunier, Samuel H. *The Irrepressible Democrat: Roger Williams.* New York, 1940.
Brown, Robert E. *Charles Beard and the Constitution.* New York, 1965.
Browne, William H. (ed.). *Archives of Maryland.* Vol. I. Baltimore, 1883.
Burnet, Thomas. *History of the Reformation.* Vol. I. London, 1865.

Bury, John. *The Moderate Christian.* London, 1611.
Busher, Leonard. *Religious Peace: or, A Plea for Liberty of Conscience.* London, 1614.
Calvin, John. *Institutes of the Christian Religion.* Philadelphia, 1960.
Canne, John. *A Light for the Ignorant.* London, 1636.
Chauncy, Charles. *The Only Compulsion Proper to Be Made Use of in the Affairs of Conscience and Religion.* Boston, 1739.
Clark, Peter. *The Rulers Highest Dignity, and the Peoples Truest Glory.* Boston, 1739.
Cobbett, William. *The Parliamentary History of England.* Vol. I. London, 1806.
Connecticut Gazette. New Haven, October, 1757.
Cragg, G. R. *From Puritanism to the Age of Reason.* Cambridge, 1966.
———. *Puritanism in the Period of the Great Persecution.* Cambridge, 1957.
Cranston, Maurice. *John Locke: A Biography.* New York, 1957.
Dod, John. *A Plain and Familiar Explanation of the Ten Commandments.* London, 1609.
Dooyeweerd, Herman. *A New Critique of Theoretical Thought.* 4 vols. Philadelphia, 1958.
Doubleday and Company. *The Constitution of the United States of America and the Declaration of Independence.* New York, n.d.
Downame, George. *The Christians Freedom.* London, 1635.
Fuller, Thomas. *The Holy and Profane State.* London, 1831.
Gales, Joseph, comp. *The Debates and Proceedings in the Congress of the United States.* Vols. I, II. Washington, 1834.
George, Charles and Katherine. *The Protestant Mind of the English Reformation, 1570-1640.* Princeton, 1961.
Goold, W. H. (ed.). *The Works of John Owen.* 24 vols. Edinburgh, 1850-1853.
Gould, George (ed.). *Documents Relating to the Settlement of the Church of England by the Act of Uniformity of 1662.* London, 1862.
Greenham, Richard. *Works.* London, 1620.
Hall, David D. (ed.). *The Antinomian Controversy, 1636-1638.* Middletown, 1968.
Hall, Joseph. *Works.* Vol. VI. London, 1863.
Haller, W., Davies, G. (eds.). *The Leveller Tracts, 1647-1653.* New York, 1944.
Haller, W. *Liberty and Reformation in the Puritan Revolution.* New York, 1955.

BIBLIOGRAPHY

Haller, William. *The Rise of Puritanism.* New York, 1958.

Harrington, James. *A System of Politics.* London, 1700.

———. *The Commonwealth of Oceana.* London, 1656.

———. *Humble Petition.* London, 1659.

———. *Valerius and Publicola.* London, 1659.

Haskins, George Lee. *Law and Authority in Early Massachusetts.* New York, 1960.

Heimert, Alan. *Religion and the American Mind: From the Great Awakening to the Revolution.* Cambridge, 1966.

Helwys, Thomas. *A Declaration of Faith.* London, 1611.

———. *A Short Declaration of the Mystery of Iniquity.* London, 1612.

Hetherington, W. M. *History of the Westminster Assembly of Divines.* Edinburgh, 1856.

Hildersam, Arthur. *CVII Lectures on the Fourth of John.* London, 1642.

Hosmer, James K. (ed.). *Winthrop's Journal.* 2 vols. New York, 1908.

Jacob, Henry. *A Confession and Protestation.* Amsterdam, 1612.

Jaeger, Werner. *Aristotle.* Oxford, 1955.

Jones, Rufus M. *The Quakers in the American Colonies.* New York, 1966.

Jordan, W. K. *The Development of Religious Toleration in England.* 4 vols. Cambridge, 1932-1940.

Kelly, Alfred H., Harbison, W. A. *The American Constitution.* New York, 1963.

Kik, J. M. "Dr. Williams Library Notebooks." Unpublished notes on material in the Williams Library. Westminster Theological Seminary Library, Philadelphia, Pa.

Leder, Lawrence. *Liberty and Authority: Early American Political Ideology, 1689-1763.* Chicago, 1968.

Locke, John. *A Letter Concerning Toleration.* Patrick Romanell, ed. New York, 1955.

Lynd, Staughton. *The Intellectual Origins of American Radicalism.* New York, 1968.

McIlwain, C. H. (ed.). *The Political Works of James I.* Cambridge, 1918.

McKeon, Richard (ed.). *The Basic Works of Aristotle.* New York, 1941.

McNeill, J. T. "Casuistry in the Puritan Age," *Religion and Life,* XII (1943), pp. 76-89.

Marsden, George M. "Perry Miller's Rehabilitation of the Puritans: A Critique," *Church History,* XXXIX (March, 1970), pp. 91-132.

Matthews, A. G. *Calamy Revised.* Oxford, 1934.

Maule, Thomas. *Tribute to Caesar.* Philadelphia, 1712.

Miller, Perry. *The New England Mind.* 2 vols. Boston, 1961.

———. *Orthodoxy in Massachusetts 1630-1650.* Cambridge, 1933.

———. *Roger Williams: His Contribution to the American Tradition.* New York, 1962.

Miller, Perry, Johnson, Thomas H. (eds.). *The Puritans: A Sourcebook of Their Writings.* New York, 1938.

Milton, John. *Works.* London, 1659.

Mitchell, A. F. (ed.). *Minutes of the Sessions of the Westminster Assembly of Divines.* London, 1874.

More, Thomas. *Utopia.* London, 1895.

Morgan, Edmund S. *Roger Williams: The Church and the State.* New York, 1967.

———. *Visible Saints: The History of a Puritan Idea.* Ithaca, 1963.

Mosse, George L. *The Holy Pretence: A Study in Christianity and Reason of State from William Perkins to John Winthrop.* London, 1957.

Neale, J. E. *Elizabeth I and Her Parliaments.* 2 vols. London, 1958.

New York Gazette. New York, February, 1753.

Occasional Reverberator. New York, October, 1753.

Ong, Walter, S. J. *Ramus, Method and the Decay of Dialogue.* Cambridge, 1958.

Overton, Richard. *The Arraignment of Mr. Persecution.* London, 1645.

Padover, Saul K. *The Complete Jefferson.* New York, 1943.

Palmer, Thomas. *An Essay of the Means How to Make Our Travels.* London, 1606.

Paul, Robert S. (ed.). *An Apologetical Narration.* Boston, 1963.

Paul, Robert S. *The Lord Protector.* London, 1955.

Pease, T. C. *The Leveller Movement.* Washington, 1916.

Pennsylvania Gazette. Philadelphia, January, 1747/48.

Perkins, William. *Works.* 3 vols. London, 1612-1618.

Petrie, George. *Church and State in Early Maryland.* Baltimore, 1892.

Pettit, Norman. *The Heart Prepared.* New Haven, 1966.

Pfeffer, Leo. *Church, State and Freedom.* Boston, 1953.

Pierce, C. A. *Conscience in the New Testament.* London, 1958.

Prince Society. *Publications.* Vol. I. Boston, 1858.

Randall, John. *Twenty-nine Lectures on the Church.* Vol. II. London, 1636.

Rhode Island Gazette. Providence, January, 1733/34.

Robinson, Henry. *Liberty of Conscience.* London, 1644.
Robinson, John. *Works.* Vol. I. London, 1851.
Rogers, Richard. *Seven Treatises [Toward] True Happiness.* London, 1610.
Rosenmeier, Jesper. "The Teacher and the Witness: John Cotton and Roger Williams," *William and Mary Quarterly,* Series 3, XXV (July, 1968), pp. 408-431.
Runes, Dagobert D. *Dictionary of Philosophy.* Ames, Iowa, 1955.
Rushworth, John. *Historical Collections.* Vol. I. London, 1659.
Russell and Russell Company. *The Complete Writings of Roger Williams.* 7 vols. New York, 1653.
Sevenster, J. N. *Paul and Seneca.* Leiden, 1961.
Shea, Daniel B., Jr. *Spiritual Autobiography in Early America.* Princeton, 1968.
Shepard, Thomas. *Works.* 3 vols. Boston, 1853.
Shurtleff, Nathaniel B. (ed.). *Records of the Governor and Company of the Massachusetts Bay in New England.* Vol. I. Boston, 1853-1854.
Smyth, John. *Confession of Faith.* London, 1611.
Spier, J. M. *An Introduction to Christian Philosophy.* Philadelphia, 1954.
Stephen Leslie, et al. (eds.). *Dictionary of National Biography.* 22 vols. London, 1882-1949.
Stevens, Benjamin. *A Sermon Preached at Boston.* Boston, 1761.
Stevenson, Joseph, et al. (eds.). *Calendars of State Papers, Domestic Series, of the Reign of Elizabeth.* London, 1865.
Tanner, E. P. *The Province of New Jersey, 1664-1738.* New York, 1908.
Thorpe, F. N. (ed.). *The Federal and State Constitutions, Colonial Charters, and Other Organic Laws.* 7 vols. Washington, 1909.
Trinterud, Leonard J. "The Origins of Puritanism," *Church History,* XX (1951), pp. 37-57.
Underhill, E. B. (ed.). *Tracts on Liberty of Conscience and Persecution.* London, 1846.
United Presbyterian Church. *Book of Confessions.* Philadelphia, 1966.
United States Government Printing Office. *Journals of the Continental Congress, 1774-1789.* Vol. IV. Washington, 1906.
Van Til, L. John. "The Appeal to Conscience," *Christianity Today,* XIII (May 23, 1969), pp. 6-8.
Visscher, Hugo. *William Ames: His Life and Works.* Douglas Horton, tr. Cambridge, 1956.
Walwyn, William. *The Compassionate Samaritan.* London, 1643.

Williams, Abraham. *A Sermon Preached at Boston.* Boston, 1762.
Windelband, W. *History of Ancient Philosophy.* New York, 1957.
Wise, John. *A Vindication of the Government of the New England Churches.* Boston, 1717.
Wood, Thomas. *English Casuistical Divinity During the Seventeenth Century.* London, 1952.
Ziff, Larzer. *The Career of John Cotton.* Princeton, 1962.
Ziff, Larzer (ed.). *John Cotton on the Churches of New England.* Cambridge, 1968.

www.ingramcontent.com/pod-product-compliance
Lightning Source LLC
LaVergne TN
LVHW010258260326
834688LV00044B/1351